THE FACE OF TEXAS

THE FACE

A Survey in Words and Pictures

With Photographs by QUINCY HOWE, JR., and Others

OF TEXAS

by GREEN PEYTON

Bonanza Books, New York

BOOKS *by* GREEN PEYTON

Information

THE FACE OF TEXAS
AMERICA'S HEARTLAND, THE SOUTHWEST
SAN ANTONIO—CITY IN THE SUN
5,000 MILES TOWARDS TOKYO

Biography

FOR GOD AND TEXAS: THE LIFE OF P. B. HILL

Novels

RAIN ON THE MOUNTAIN
BLACK CABIN

This edition is published by Bonanza Books,
a division of Crown Publishers, Inc.,
by arrangement with Thomas Y. Crowell Company.

Copyright © 1961 by Green Peyton

Designed by Edwin Kaplin

Manufactured in the United States of America

Library of Congress Catalog Card No. 61-10483

Title page picture by Lynwood Abram

1 2 3 4 5 6 7 8 9 10

This book is dedicated to
CLAIRE PERRY
and to the memory of
GEORGE SESSIONS PERRY
who was a Texan,
a fine writer,
and an excellent friend

CONTENTS

San Jacinto Monument
on the battlefield near Houston

1: This Is Texas

The Alamo

IN San Antonio there is a department store bearing the eloquent name, Joske's of Texas. It is only a few yards down the street, past the old Menger Hotel, from the most hallowed shrine of Texas liberty; and so naturally it uses the address, By the Alamo.

Several years ago, Joske's of Texas replaced the motto by which it had been known as long as anybody could remember. It had been "the biggest store in the biggest state." Now it is known with becoming simplicity as "the greatest store in the greatest state."

It is hard to tell whether an unexpected rush of modesty brought about the change, or whether it was suggested by some alteration in the store's commercial rank. Maybe it was learned, for example, that Foley's in Houston was bigger. Whatever the reason, revising its motto turned out to be a display of remarkable prescience by Joske's. For regardless of the size of the store today, Texas no longer is the biggest state. Since January 3, 1959, Alaska is.

The admission of Alaska to the Union was perhaps a blessing that few Texans noticed at the time. A great many jokes used to be made about the cult of bigness in Texas. Most of them were unprintable, and nearly all were seasoned with more than a trace of rancor toward the typically Texan traits of optimism, candor, and self-confidence.

The jokes are made no longer. But Texas is as big as ever. In many respects, it is bigger.

Figures do not show its full size. From the western tip of Texas, on the middle reaches of the Rio Grande near El Paso, to the eastern edge at the Sabine River, next to Louisiana, is almost exactly 775 miles as a jet flies. From the southern tip near Brownsville, at the mouth of the Rio Grande, to the northwest corner of the Panhandle is a round 800 miles.

It helps you to visualize the distances if you imagine that Texas could be laid out on the eastern half of the United States, between the Mississippi River and the Atlantic Ocean. Supposing that Texarkana were placed on the site of Baltimore, El Paso would be where St. Louis is. Brownsville would become Savannah, Georgia; and at the top of the Panhandle you would find Grand Rapids, Michigan.

Transposed to the East this way, Texas would cover most of Kentucky, Ohio, North and South Carolina, West Virginia, and Virginia; much of Georgia, Tennessee, and Indiana; parts of Illinois, Michigan, Maryland, and Pennsylvania; not to mention a small piece of Ontario,

Joske's in San Antonio

Canada. Yet comparisons of this kind mean little, because the extent of a place can be measured by other quantities than miles.

The bigness of Texas is in the land itself. Everywhere the earth is level, wide, and open, stretching away and away, under the vast panoply of the sky. Visitors may very well find it tedious, as one apparently featureless expanse dissolves into the next one. But, to a Texan, the immensity signifies freedom, the seeming emptiness is room for action, space for movement and for growth.

People in other places feel strongly about Texas, whether they are for it or against it. If you doubt this, try making your way through traffic around Washington or New York in an automobile with a Texas license. Drivers who ordinarily roll along the highway in a state of high good temper, unaffected by citizens from Montana or Mississippi, are roused into a fever of competition at the sight of a car from Texas. They are compelled to overtake and pass it, by a passion stronger than themselves.

When a Texan attends a meeting in Los Angeles or Chicago, the chairman is likely to recognize him by reciting one of those bawdy tales about the inhabitants of Texas. There are travelers who go for miles in any direction to avoid passing through Texas. And there are pilgrims who keep returning to it, as if drawn by some mystical attraction which they cannot define.

Various qualities in Texas and its citizens contribute to this strength of feeling. On the debit side of the ledger, the one most often mentioned

4 is the character of the land itself—its apparent monotony, which may repel natives of a more picturesque region. On the credit side is the fact that, to nearly all Americans, Texas represents the eternal frontier—the old West of cattle drives, pioneer women, and men quick on the draw.

The legend of life on the plains is perhaps the most enduring myth in the mind of our nation. It depicts our view of ourselves and our aspirations, as the Homeric legend once gave an image of their intrinsic nature to the civilized inhabitants of Greece. Of course the frontier no longer exists, even in Texas. But the myth—and its identification with some personal trait in each of us—persists.

Another explanation for the response that Texas manages to excite is the reputation it has today of being rich. According to our own circumstances, we are inclined to look upon it with envy, exasperation, or longing to share its bounty. Texas is supposed to be a place where every homesteader has an oil well in his back yard and drives a Cadillac.

There is some truth in this fantasy. All Texans obviously aren't rich. But Texas is fabulously endowed with natural resources, and every Texan believes that he *can* be rich, with a reasonable amount of luck. Meanwhile, he may indeed drive a Cadillac, because it costs only a few dollars more a month, and Texans—rich or poor—like to feel that what they have is the best. That is why quite ordinary Texans often stay at the lordly Shamrock Hotel in Houston, or dine and drink in Galveston's brilliant Balinese Room, or buy clothes for their wives at Neiman-Marcus in Dallas —which makes quite a point of the fact that all its merchandise, while smart, is not necessarily expensive.

From living—sometimes recklessly—on their expansive and not always predictable land, Texans have learned a truth that frequently eludes more cautious people in other parts of the world. It is that handsome things, which uplift the human spirit with a fleeting sense of luxury and ease, can be had by anybody on occasion—if only by sacrificing some of the routine comforts of daily existence—and they are worth it.

Besides, in Texas the routine comforts cost less than in some other places, as a U. S. Department of Labor survey showed a while back.

And so, wherever you travel by car in Texas, you find lavish motor hotels like the Western Hills in Fort Worth—which is more than merely a pleasant place to spend the night. For a population as mobile as Arabs, that sees nothing exceptional in driving a hundred miles for dinner, a hostelry such as the Western Hills is a kind of suburban club, with its own swimming pool, specialty shop, and dining rooms in which the service is more cosmopolitan than cow-town.

6   These are not pleasures enjoyed solely by the rich. On the contrary, the typical patrons are more likely a couple whose home is a nondescript ranch house somewhere in a grove of mesquite.

In whatever way they live at home, when Texans journey beyond the far-flung borders of their state, they prefer to go in style. They take with them that cheerful air of satisfaction with all things Texan, which may seem an affront to people elsewhere. It is not so intended. Texans are deeply imbued with the ideal of independence. They want to be—and feel that they are—self-sufficient. One of the reasons they travel abroad is to reassure themselves that Texas is doing all right.

The urge to be free is what makes them manage their own oil production, through the Railroad Commission which was created almost three-quarters of a century ago to regulate their own transportation system. It is why they also have made laws favoring insurance companies chartered in Texas—not always, to be sure, with the most fortunate results. Texas—though it acknowledges a kind of dominion status within the Union—has carried on a campaign of long standing to preserve its condition as a separate social and economic entity.

Ladies shopping at Neiman-Marcus

ncy Howe, Jr.

The San Jacinto River

It has even managed to extend its influence well outside its own territory. For example, there was the rousing proxy battle a few years ago, in which the late Robert R. Young, from Texas, won control of the New York Central Railroad. He did it with the help of $20,000,000 in stock, bought by his Texas friends, Clint Murchison—whose financial interests reach into places far removed from Texas—and the late Sid Richardson.

8   According to intimates of Richardson, after the deal was arranged, he called Murchison on the telephone to ask: "Clint, what was the name of that railroad we just bought?"

For a good illustration of the authority that Texas has been known to wield outside its boundaries, one need only cast a quick glance at the recent composition of the United States government. Its President for eight years was Dwight D. Eisenhower, a native of Denison, Texas, though he grew up in Kansas. The Speaker of the House of Representatives, for the best part of two decades, has been Sam Rayburn, of Bonham, Texas. The Majority Leader of the Senate—our nearest equivalent in power and prestige to a Prime Minister—was Lyndon Baines Johnson, of Stonewall, Texas, until he became Vice-President.

The election that gave him this office was largely won by Johnson's influence over the neighboring South—and by his firm hand on his own state.

There was a time, during the spring of 1960, when Lyndon Johnson struck many people as a more likely candidate for President than the man who finally got the nomination, and later assumed the office. Two fateful decisions faced the Majority Leader in those months before the election. The first was whether to risk his place in the Senate by trying for the top office in the land.

As luck would have it, 1960 was the year when Senator Johnson had to decide whether he would run for re-election to the seat once occupied by Sam Houston. If he did, nobody doubted that he would win it. But there was also the possibility that he might be nominated for President.

Suffolk sheep in the Hill Country

Quincy Howe,

incy Howe, Jr.

State Capitol at end of Congress Avenue, Austin

Governor Price Daniel

Bill Malone

10   If he withdrew from the Senate campaign, and then failed to win the presidential nomination, Lyndon Johnson would be out of a job, and Texas would be deprived of its most persuasive voice in Washington.

The Legislature took care of that question. They fixed it so that Johnson could run for both offices at the same time. That way, they figured, if he missed a chance to become the No. 1 man in the nation, he would still be No. 2, the Majority Leader.

The second decision faced by the senator that year was at the Demo-

Vice-President Lyndon Johnson with President Kennedy at the LBJ Ranch

cratic National Convention, when his successful opponent, John F. Kennedy, offered him the nomination as Vice-President. If he accepted, and won, he would be giving up the second most powerful elective office in the United States for the rather nebulous authority of the President's understudy and the Senate's presiding deity. As everybody now knows, he did accept, and won, by the same microscopic plurality that President Kennedy received over Richard M. Nixon.

Opposing Johnson for the Senate in the same campaign was a diminutive, earnest Republican professor of political science from Wichita Falls, John G. Tower. The 926,000 votes that Tower rolled up were still not enough to take Johnson's seat away from him.

But Johnson then resigned, so that he could assume the office of Vice-President. In the special election that followed, to fill the Senate vacancy, Tower first led a record field of seventy candidates, and then won the run-off over conservative Democrat William A. Blakley, the temporary incumbent appointed by Governor Daniel. Thus John Tower became the first Republican Senator from Texas in modern times

It has been observed that the 9,500,000 people of Texas often exert more weight in national councils than in their own. Texans are mighty independent when it comes to the management of affairs at home. But when people who aren't Texans oppose them, in matters which affect their pride, they can be headstrong, obstinate, and singularly unanimous.

The rest of the country found that out shortly after World War II, when it was agitated by the question of the Texas tidelands. This complicated issue went back to the days when Texas was a colony of Spain. Under Spanish law, its offshore boundaries extended into the Gulf of Mexico for a distance of three leagues, or a little more than ten miles.

The Texas Constitution, which was accepted by the United States in 1845, when Texas joined the Union, recognized the old Spanish land titles, along with those of the Mexican government and the Republic of Texas, which had inherited the sovereignty of Spain. In solitary splendor among the states, Texas also retained possession of its own public lands—including the ones in the Gulf.

Nobody bothered much about the submerged territory off the coast until a century later. Then it was discovered not only that the 4,000 square miles of Texas tidelands had oil under them, but that the savory fluid could be recovered, by drilling from platforms raised above the water.

The United States promptly sued for ownership of the sunken prairie, on the ground that Texas had automatically lost title to it by entering the

12   Union. The Supreme Court upheld this view in 1950, over the wrathful protestations of Price Daniel, then the Attorney General of Texas.

But Texans remembered the Alamo, whose defenders had been wiped out in March 1836, and thought of San Jacinto, where six weeks later Sam Houston had fallen on the forces of Mexican General Santa Anna, and had won all of this land for Texas. While the United Nations fought in Korea, and the Rosenbergs were being condemned to death for selling atomic secrets, the campaign for the tidelands went on in the halls of Congress. Twice bills were passed, giving them back to Texas. Each time, President Truman vetoed the bill, and not enough votes could be mustered to override the veto.

Then Dwight D. Eisenhower was nominated for President by the Republican party, and Adlai Stevenson by the Democrats. Price Daniel and the other Texas leaders asked one question of each candidate: Did he support the claim of Texas to the tidelands? Governor Stevenson said, "No." General Eisenhower said, "Yes." He was elected.

It would be going too far to say that President Eisenhower won because he favored the return of the tidelands to Texas. There were some other issues in the campaign of 1952. But that was the only one of any interest to most Texans. For the second time in history, a Republican candidate for President carried the state. The first time had been back in 1928, when Herbert Hoover had won over liquor and Catholicism.

In the same election, Price Daniel was rewarded for his zeal with a seat in the United States Senate. It was the one abdicated by courtly old Tom Connally, who was more concerned about foreign affairs than about oil. Price Daniel introduced another bill—the third one—giving the tidelands back to Texas. It passed again, and this time the President signed it.

That was evidently all Senator Daniel wanted in Washington. He spent four years of his six-year term fretting all the time for Texas. In 1956 he went home and ran for governor. He came in just ahead of a moderately liberal former judge from Austin, Ralph Yarborough. Judge Yarborough then ran in a special election for Governor Daniel's seat in the Senate. He won without any trouble.

In spite of its defection to Hoover in 1928, Texas has long been considered a western outpost of the Solid South. Most Texans are born into the Democratic party, as Roman Catholics are born into the Church and some New Englanders are born into an appropriate class at Harvard.

There is more than a possibility—judging by the returns—that many Texans may have changed their political allegiance permanently in the campaigns of 1952, 1956, and 1960. If so, they were moved less by so-

Quincy Howe, Jr.

Laredo High School

cial and religious fervor than is ordinarily assumed in circles that continue to associate Texas with the Confederacy, and more by economic interests like the tidelands, which are indigenous to the state.

The question of liquor hasn't come up in a national election since Herbert Hoover's day. If it had, Texans would probably have taken it in stride. A goodly number of the Fundamentalist farmers who once looked on drinking as a sin now live in the city and give cocktail parties for their friends. On the whole, Texas is satisfied with the present law that forbids the sale of spirits by the drink in public places. Besides, an arid waste survives in the hinterlands, where not even a glass of beer can be bought legally.

The question of Catholicism *did* come up in 1960. Candidate Kennedy gave it a thorough airing before a church group in Houston. He was able to convince at least a few Protestant Texans that the Pope wouldn't be lurking behind an arras in the White House, telling him what to do.

Liquor and religion are matters of personal taste. Texans generally are inclined to let them flourish in privacy. But oil is something else again. Liquid petroleum is a sustenance that courses through the arteries of Texas. The latter-day economy of the state is largely nourished by it.

The question of oil came up, too, in the campaign of 1960. This time the issue was the 27½ per cent allowance for depletion which the Internal Revenue Service grants on income from oil and gas production, and which the Democratic platform threatened to reduce or repeal. It was Lyndon Johnson who convinced enough Texans that President Kennedy would overlook that particular landmark on the New Frontier.

The argument over depletion made less noise than the argument over Kennedy's faith. But the chances are that it had more to do with the fact that Texas very nearly went Republican again in 1960. Only about 60 per cent of the churchgoing people of Texas are Protestant. But almost everybody is affected in some way by the petroleum industry.

Texas in recent years has become one of a half-dozen crucial states in national elections. Politicians would do well to remember that, when they get to thinking tenderly of the taxes lost on depletion, or of the sunken revenues in the tidelands.

As it happens, the tidelands of Texas are neither as easily accessible nor as productive as the offshore lands of neighboring Louisiana, which also were restored in 1953. But they have been profitable for the State Treasury, all the same. Up to June 1957—the last time any figures were publicly available—a total of ninety-eight wells had been drilled off the coast of Texas. Of these, nine were then producing.

Revenues from the public lands of Texas are paid into a permanent fund to help support the public school system. Through April 1957, the income received by the fund from leases on the tidelands added up to nearly $63,000,000. The total amount of the fund that year was $360,-000,000. By 1959, it had grown to $396,550,000.

Because of this provision in the Constitution, the Texas school system as a whole is one of the most richly endowed institutions in the country. Except for rare and grudging dispensations, it is allowed to spend nothing but the income on the fund. However, the schools draw expense money from a variety of other state, county, and district taxes. Altogether, Texas lavished $701,000,000 on education for its 2,001,531 children of school age in 1957–58. It worked out to $429 worth of teaching for each of the 1,635,000 pupils who regularly attended public schools. The national average, mostly from taxes, was about $464.

Even so, life in Texas doesn't consist solely in the delightful task of figuring out how to squander royalties from oil leases. There are public and private dissensions, financial troubles, altercations, calamities, and plain cussedness enough to keep the passing hours from getting dreary.

Among the living writers of Texas, none have expressed its charm with more natural fluency than Frank Dobie and Stanley Walker. Nor could two men, both endowed with keen perceptions, see their homeland more differently.

Dobie is a son of cattlemen, who sent himself to college, took a master's degree in English, taught literature at the University of Texas off and on for thirty-three years, wrote books haunted by the spell of the plains, and became a liberal (some Texans would say a radical) Democrat, with a benign distaste for high-handed reactionaries.

Walker was a country boy who went east, became a hard-bitten, cantankerous newspaperman, was city editor of the New York *Herald Tribune,* wrote a couple of books about Manhattan, and returned—a rock-ribbed Republican—to the farm which his father had saved for him near Lampasas, to raise turkeys and compose dispatches, with the sharp eye of a veteran reporter, on events in Texas.

One evening in the summer of 1959, Stanley Walker sent a story to the *Herald Tribune* relating some of the difficulties that were facing Governor Daniel. Nothing ever written about Texas yields its flavor any better. Datelined Austin, it went like this:

The other evening a small group of Texas lawmakers and lobbyists were sitting at a table in the dimly lit dining room of the tastefully decorated and remodeled old Driskill Hotel. . . . They were discussing a history-making bill, just signed by the Governor, which would set up a sort of vague machinery for "advertising Texas. . . ."

Frank Dobie with Stanley Walker

United Press International

Quincy Howe, Jr.

Oil refinery at Texas City

18 The legislation setting up this body has been sharply attacked on several grounds—one being that . . . the great, rich State of Texas has no money to spend for advertising or anything else. A special session of the Legislature now is trying to find a way of meeting a deficit of more than $65,000,000 (the banks are honoring the hot checks given to State employes) and to find something like $300,000,000 to finance Government operations over the next two years. . . .

The conferees were interrupted by a gray-haired, thoughtful old gentleman, well known in Texas, who was at the next table. "May I ask," inquired this scholarly killjoy, "just what it is about Texas that you intend to advertise?" He went on roughly as follows:

"You might, of course, advertise that we have superb floods and terrifying droughts. . . . You might also allude to the fact that scores of the smaller Texas municipalities are withering away, their population and business being taken over by the larger cities. . . .

The San Antonio River

Quincy Howe,

Quincy Howe, Jr.

Yoking a steer in the Stockyards at San Angelo

"You might say something about the homicide rate, especially in Houston;
. . . the crowded prisons and substandard jails; the inadequate library facilities;
the insurance and land scandals; . . . the prevalence of loan sharks; the depletion of some of the State's best agricultural land; the hard fried cow steaks;
the awful mortality on the highways; the medical quacks; the fact that more
than half the counties are dry; and——"

"Un-Texan!" yelped a wounded legislator.

"Not at all," said the old realist. "I love Texas. Nice folks. Good sunsets
now and then. More quail this year than I ever saw. The Gulf shrimp is good."

What the aged patriot was really saying was that the principal point about
Texas at the moment is not its glory, but its besetting problems. Solve them,
and the boosting will take care of itself. Besides, there is a sneaking notion in
many quarters that the State of Texas needs advertising about as badly as
Bennett Cerf needs a press agent.

From the inexorable piling up of issues, in this account, toward its
mournful climax—"the fact that more than half the counties are dry—"
you might be justified in concluding that Texas at this moment is a pretty
unrewarding place to live. On the contrary, it is—for those who like it—
a most excellent place to live. One reason is that nobody in Texas takes
murmurings like these too seriously. Every habitation has its drawbacks.

Texas bears its burdens either with pride—because, like the vagaries of the weather, they are more spectacular than in other parts—or with wry amusement, as quirks of nature in an otherwise satisfying land.

If you examine the problems that Stanley Walker cites, they turn out in most cases to be the common vexations of our time. Local governments everywhere find themselves financially embarrassed, because the cost of all the services that governments provide has gone up, and the Federal Director of Internal Revenue takes the first big cut out of everybody's income. Country folk are moving into cities—and then out to the suburbs—all over the civilized world, in Australia as well as in Texas. Homicide rates are high, prisons are crowded, and death is a familiar incident on the highways, simply because there are more people.

Statistics of this kind are more noticeable in Texas, partly on account of the fact that it has matured so quickly, and in part because the citizens of Texas are accustomed to doing as they please—a habit that frequently brings them into casual contact with the law. The contact is casual, because the law in Texas harks back to the frontier, where the marshal was primarily interested in seeing that things were done according to the rules—that you didn't shoot a man in the back, for instance, or put poison in his well. So long as you observe these niceties in Texas, what you do is your own business. You explain it to the officer, he fills out a report, and you go on your way. Nowhere on earth—except perhaps in England—are policemen so discreet as in Texas.

Indeed, politeness—of a soft-spoken, often uncommunicative kind—is one of the notable characteristics of Texans in their own environment. This too is a survival of frontier manners. You don't insult a man in Texas, unless you intend to kill him—or are prepared to have him kill you. Paradoxically, the imminent possibility of violence on the plains promotes a rather peculiar sense of personal security. If you have no quarrel with anybody, you are not likely to be bothered. Petty thievery and mayhem are less prevalent than in most other regions of the world—for the obvious reason that they are also grounds for shooting. Where sudden death is the accepted penalty for making trouble, the incidence of homicide may rise, but the chance of being disturbed in other ways is less.

Just as Texas has—in its own way—this preference for a rather wary social order, so it leans toward an orderly appearance in its landscape and its institutions. The very fact that so much of the countryside itself tends to be sober and severe may encourage this bent among its people. There is nothing exuberant or intense about the natural environment of Texas. It doesn't run to somber swamps or pensive bayous, as in nearby Louisi-

…incy Howe, Jr.

Picking cotton near Lubbock

ana; or to the lush tropical valleys of Mexico, beyond the Rio Grande; or to blazing deserts or imposing mountains like the austere lands toward the Pacific.

The forests of East Texas are neither vast nor particularly primeval. Instead they are sedately wooded. The coastal plain is bare, brown, and level; to the south, the lowlands are covered by mesquite thickets; and in the west are long, tilted slopes, broken by small sierras and discreet cañons. Everywhere the prospect is a moderate one, neither luxuriant nor barren—stupendous nor common—rugged nor serene—but infinitely varied in subdued gradations. Texas is the only great area on the North American continent whose features are always temperate. Beside it, other regions invariably look extreme.

Whether for this reason or for some other, the inhabitants of Texas have taken care not to disturb its composure. Their homes are generally inconspicuous—even drab—blending into the staid aspect of the terrain. Only in public resorts do they enjoy ostentation. The towns are neat, embellished with modern buildings, and clean. There are few billboards along the highways in Texas. But there are many roadside parks, fitted out with stone picnic tables and barbecue pits, in groves of trees or under rustic shelters in the hills or on the plains. In these outdoor dining pavilions, Texas families pause to rest and admire the greatness of Texas around them, ignoring—and ignored by—other Texans passing on.

Texas highways, on the whole, are exceptionally handsome and easy to travel. Wide, level—or with gentle grades in hilly country—covered with tar and asphalt on which cars roll effortlessly at eighty miles an hour, they are bordered by broad shoulders that encourage parking. The view beside them is always distant, changing in subtle ways, but seldom startling.

The Highway Department takes pains to landscape its thoroughfares —not necessarily to impress visitors, but to please the inhabitants who travel on them most. In South Texas they are lined with palms, on the parched plains in the west by cactus, and with grass and waving wildflowers wherever they will grow. Texans live on wheels, as they once lived on horseback. Nothing delights a Texan more than to be out in the open, tooling across the prairie, contemplating the endless miles of Texas, unfolding one by one before him.

This is one of the paradoxes of the state—that so much has been done to bring comfort and esthetic satisfaction to an essentially unrewarding ground. For nothing that Texas provides from its soil is easy to come by—not even oil, which flows so bountifully when you find it, but so often

24 isn't found. Crops are coaxed out of fields that are normally too dry or too moist, or better suited to grass. Industries are raised on deserted pastures without coal or raw materials or enough running water.

Yet Texas is, above all things, a civilized domain—not in the prim way of a New England town, or the polished way of a Virginia hunt club, or the spectacular way of a California suburb, but civilized nonetheless, in its own plain-speaking, unpretentious style. Its culture is founded on the social economy of isolated ranches, where the amenities of life had to be—and were—freighted in laboriously by river boat or oxcart or rail.

The seeming emptiness and monotony of these level reaches were noted a while back. To a visitor passing through Texas, they appear as the most fundamental aspect of the state. Yet they are only apparent. Among the wonders of Texas, to those who know it well, is its unending diversity. It starts with the manifold character of the land itself, beneath its look of conformity: changing almost imperceptibly from the cypress-bordered lakes and piney woods of East Texas to brown prairies around Dallas and Fort Worth; from the shallow bays and sandy beaches along

Sand dunes at Padre Island

Landscape on the High Plains

26 the Gulf Coast to the rocky meadows and cedar brakes in the Hill Country; from the tumbled crests of the mountains west of the Pecos to the flat, high plains above the Cap Rock in the Panhandle.

Whatever the nature of the ground, in whatever part of Texas, there are unexpected clumps of cottonwood or juniper or live oak along river beds and in hidden valleys. Lakes are found in improbable places, surrounded sometimes by bare hills or arid brush; and, where they enclose water in its impatient course toward the Gulf, there will be inland sailboats, motor launches, people swimming, basking on floats, or wading or fishing along the shores.

On this varied ground has grown a profusion of unlikely industry and impetuous agriculture. Not only is Texas covered from one end to the other with oil shafts, extracting liquid energy from vast pools under the earth, and with cattle, grazing on the lean grass above it. Also Texas is the home of a great chemical crucible, concocting odd materials and exotic fuels for the space age; of enormous aircraft plants, tool forges and instrument shops, and manufacturing plants of many different kinds.

Texas produces a third of the nation's cotton, and more total food crops than any other state. Its nine major ports—and several smaller ones—handle more shipping than those of any other maritime state except New York. A metallic web of pipe lines reaches out from Texas in all directions, carrying natural gas to the homes and industries of other areas. In fact, these once-neglected plains, where the buffalo and Indians roamed, are today among the busiest and most productive regions on our planet.

It is that Texas—not the TV version—that this book celebrates.

2: San Antonio— The Old Garrison

vey Belgin—San Antonio Light

The River as the Spaniards saw it

*T*HE story of Texas properly begins in San Antonio. It begins there because—from the great sweep of country which was Texas yesterday, and is Texas today—this is the point that was chosen for settlement, first by Spaniards, tracking a tentative route across the plains out of Mexico, and later by Anglo-Saxons from the United States.

San Antonio was founded more than 240 years ago, which makes it the oldest center of culture in Texas. The towns of Ysleta, Socorro, and San Elizario, along the Rio Grande south of El Paso, were established earlier. But they were really offshoots of New Mexico, and were little more than chapels in the wilderness. San Antonio is the genesis from which Texas grew. It remains the proudest relic of Texas history.

Quincy Howe, Jr.

Mexican craftsman at La Villita

San Antonio—The Old Garrison

It became the original capital of Texas for the simplest of reasons. It had water in abundance, bubbling up out of the ground, to form a river that appeared from nowhere and meandered off to the southeast toward the Gulf of Mexico, 150 miles away.

Over all the dry and dusty stretch of land which the Spaniards had covered from San Juan Bautista, where they crossed the Rio Grande, this was the first place that appealed to them as a natural site for a home, surrounded by groves of crooked live oak, stout hackberry, and shimmering cottonwood. In the immense wasteland of Texas, tenanted only by game and a few shabby Indians, Yanaguana—as the place was called—offered itself eloquently for habitation.

In fact, San Antonio is provided by nature with the most seductive setting for a city in Texas. Though it lacks many of the economic resources of Houston or Dallas, its intrinsic advantages make it an inviting spot in which to live. On a geographical intersection dividing the four quarters of Texas, it enjoys some of the qualities of each.

San Antonio marks the boundary where the rich black prairies of East Texas end, in their long climb from the Gulf. Toward the west, the hills rise up onto the wide Edwards Plateau, where sheep and goats browse in the sun. It is from the porous limestone under the plateau that San Antonio draws its nearly inexhaustible supply of subterranean water.

A café on the River

icy Howe, Jr.

To the north, San Antonio is on the fringe of the prosperous commercial district of Texas, around Dallas. Its climate belongs to the semi-tropical south, where irrigation produces the rich truck and citrus crops of the Winter Garden and the Lower Rio Grande Valley. Banana trees rattle their broad leaves in San Antonio; palms line some of its older streets; azaleas, hibiscus, and mimosa bloom on its lawns and in its gardens. The languid temperament of San Antonio people derives from the Latin republic below the border.

This is as it should be—for civilization came to San Antonio, and so eventually to Texas, out of Mexico. It was brought by a soldier and a priest, with their troops, their monks and artisans, on the spring morning of May 1, 1718.

The soldier was Don Martín de Alarcón, newly appointed governor of Texas. The priest was Father Antonio de San Buenaventura Olivares, of the Order of St. Francis. A difference of opinion had arisen between them, shortly after their departure from Monclova, Mexico. They had divided the men and the animals between them, and kept their parties separated on the march.

At the headwaters of the San Antonio River they parted company. On a level strip of ground west of the river, beside what is now San Pedro Creek, Don Martín set about building a small fort. He called it the Presidio of Béjar (pronounced "*Bay*-har" in Spanish) for the Duke de Béjar, who was then Prince of the Asturias and would become King Ferdinand VI of Spain.

Father Antonio rested for a time in an abandoned Indian hut, organizing his forces. Then he went over to the other side of the river, half a mile from the fort, and started building a Church mission to civilize the Indians and teach them the arts of agriculture. He named it San Antonio de Valero, in honor of the saint, the river, and also the Marqués de Valero, who was Viceroy of Mexico.

Long afterwards—for reasons which are now obscure—the mission became known as The Alamo, from the word which means "cottonwood" in Spanish. Inside the stout walls of a three-acre compound, it enclosed a chapel (which is all that remains of The Alamo today) and later a small hospital, a granary, quarters for the monks and artisans, and huts for the Indian converts.

Don Martín's fort was laid out around a quadrangle which became the Plaza de Armas, or Military Plaza. (The gray limestone City Hall of San Antonio looms in the middle of it today.) Between the Presidio and the mission a straggling pueblo of adobe houses grew up along a dusty road, winding beside a bend in the river. It housed some of the officers who had acquired Indian wives, the shops of the artisans attached to the fort, and a musty *cantina* or two. A remnant of this inconspicuous village has been restored, along with some later accretions. It is called La Villita —"The Little Town."

By a polite compromise that included both the Presidio of Béjar and Mission San Antonio de Valero, the town was called San Antonio de Béjar by Spaniards in colonial times. Mexicans changed the spelling of Béjar to Béxar, which has approximately the same sound. And Bexar (pronounced by Anglo-Saxons "Bear") became the title of the present county of which San Antonio is the major part. It is a never-ending source of amusement to visitors.

The successful founding of this minute settlement in the middle of Texas—and especially Father Antonio's winning work with the Indians around the countryside—attracted other missions to the neighborhood. The first, in 1720, was Mission San José y San Miguel de Aguayo—now generally known as Mission San José. It was followed in 1731 by three more: Nuestra Señora de la Purísima Concepción de María de Acuña (or Mission Concepción), San Francisco de la Espada, and San Juan Capistrano. They were strung out down the river for a distance of eight miles from The Alamo, and linked together by an elaborate system of irrigation ditches.

The largest of the missions was San José. Its ornate domed church was constructed over a mound of packed earth, which was then dug out by hand and carted away, leaving the hollow dome. With a belfry tower seventy-five feet high, it was a landmark rising above the trees and brush for many miles across the level plains. Also it was a community more impressive than the pueblo which had brought it there in the first place.

San José was built around a broad enclosure like the one at The Alamo. On the inner side of its buttressed outer wall were rows of cells, occupied by the Indian artisans, farmers, and fighting men, whom the monks trained in their duties to God and the king. According to Father José de Solís, who described the mission in 1768, it housed about 350 heads of families; and more could be sheltered inside the walls in an emergency. The friars were housed in cloisters behind the church.

Adjoining the plaza at San José were a stone mill, turned by water from the *acequias*—the irrigation ditches—which the monks themselves had engineered, and a granary that normally held at least 5,000 bushels of corn. Down the river, some thirty miles away, San José operated a ranch with 1,500 head of cattle and 5,000 sheep and goats.

Children play in the ruined cloisters of San José Mission

Bolívar Library at La Villita

34

A walk along the River

Not only was San José the greatest missionary center of its kind in the New World; its produce also supplied all the other towns and missions in the vicinity—including San Antonio. The good fathers even shipped wine to Spain.

The later missions were somewhat less elaborate. Concepción—the nearest to the pueblo—contained a church almost as imposing as the one at San José. But it was not of the same cultural or economic importance. San Juan Capistrano and San Francisco de la Espada were smaller and more remote from the town. Their chapels were modeled on the rural churches of Mexico. They had simple whitewashed walls, and were adorned inside with painted statues of the Holy Family and the saints.

The same year that these missions were established brought a fresh infusion of people to San Antonio. Ever since the founding of the Presidio, Spain had been looking for a way to give the community some permanence. After a year or two in the wilderness, the soldiers who manned the garrison would get homesick for the towns and fertile valleys of the Sierra Madre in Mexico, and would slip away, taking their Indian wives and children with them.

The king was persuaded that it would be a sensible idea to send a group of Spanish colonists to settle this outpost on the frontier. He looked around for a place having much the same climate, in one of the other territories of Spain, as a source for the settlers. It was found in the Canary Islands, off the western bulge of Africa.

A number of indigent fishermen and workers in the Canaries, with their families, were induced to volunteer for emigration to Texas. They were transported by sea to Veracruz, and then on foot—by way of Mexico City, Saltillo, Monclova, and San Juan Bautista—to San Antonio. The fifty-five survivors of this arduous expedition arrived in March 1731.

As a reward for their enterprise, they were granted the privileges of *hidalgos*—literally, "sons of somebody," or people of distinction—and given land around the Presidio for cultivation. They built a new town of their own, called San Fernando, in honor of the same Prince of the Asturias whose name had been adopted earlier by the garrison.

The name did not endure, but the town did. In time it absorbed both the pueblo by the river and the mission called The Alamo at the other end of the village. The most impressive feature of the new town was the Church of San Fernando, completed over the next two decades on a plaza of its own, beside the fort. So substantially was the church constructed that it became a part of the present cathedral, erected in 1873 as the seat of the Catholic archbishop of San Antonio. Another relic of the Canary

Quincy Howe, Jr.

Islanders is the Spanish Governor's Palace on the Military Plaza, with its handsome patio.

The era in which San Antonio was dominated by these busy Church communities lasted only until 1794, when the missions (including The Alamo) were secularized. Their cultivated lands were then distributed among the Indians, and most of their buildings were abandoned. Over the next century and a half, while the stone churches were well preserved in the dry air, the adobe living quarters gradually crumbled and were overgrown by brush.

Mission San José has been carefully restored, except for the cloisters. It is maintained as a National Historic Site. The church of Mission Concepción and the chapels of the other missions have been rebuilt and reconsecrated.

After it ceased to be a mission colony, The Alamo was taken over by the military garrison of San Antonio, replacing the old fort. With its stout wall, its storerooms for supplies, and its monastic living quarters, it made an excellently austere habitation for soldiers. Because of the strength that Father Antonio had built into it, The Alamo was now about to become a scene of military violence, and a symbol of courage for the inhabitants of Texas.

With the Revolution of 1821 in Mexico, San Antonio passed out of the hands of Spain and became a Mexican town. It was then one of only three established communities in what is now Texas. The others were Goliad, on the San Antonio River toward the Gulf, and Nacogdoches, over in East Texas near the Louisiana border. Altogether, there were not more than 7,000 people living around these isolated centers. The frontier province was a long way from the seat of government in Mexico City, and communication between them was sketchy.

In August of that year an Anglo-American colonizer, Stephen F. Austin, arrived in San Antonio. He made arrangements with the Mexican government to let 300 families from the United States settle in Texas, and found them land on the Colorado and the Brazos Rivers, some fifty miles west of present-day Houston. Other immigrants followed them. By 1836 the population of Texas had grown to well over 35,000 people, in closer touch with the United States than with Mexico.

The President of Mexico at that time was the flamboyant General Antonio López de Santa Anna. When relations with the northern province of Texas began to deteriorate, and talk of independence was heard— among the Latins as well as the Anglo-Saxons—Santa Anna organized an army of 5,000 men and took command of it himself. He marched north, over the route of Don Martín de Alarcón, 118 years earlier, to assert his authority over the rebellious colonists.

The Alamo was in the hands of a small party of 183 volunteers, who had seized it from the President's brother-in-law, General Martín Perfecto de Cos. They were led by Colonel William Barret Travis, Jim Bowie, and the redoubtable Davy Crockett.

It is not the purpose of this book to recount the story of The Alamo. It has been told many times before. Here it is sufficient to recall that at daybreak on March 6, 1836—four days after Texas had declared its independence—Santa Anna's men swarmed over the walls, captured the old mission, killed every man in it, and burned their bodies. Santa Anna then headed east, in the direction of Goliad, where he repeated the massacre.

Only the chapel of the original Alamo—rebuilt several times—now remains to mark this high point in San Antonio history. It is revered by Texans as the sanctuary of their freedom—even though its siege ended in defeat—for two excellent reasons. One is that its little garrison of untrained men, who could have escaped, chose instead to die in its defense. The other is that it became, with Goliad, the rallying cry for Sam Houston's improvised force of 800 citizen-soldiers, when they met Santa Anna six weeks later at the San Jacinto River, on the outskirts of the present city of Houston.

There, on the afternoon of April 21, while the Mexican Army was cooking dinner and its General was enjoying a siesta, the Texans swooped down on him, shouting, "Remember The Alamo! Remember Goliad!" When the fighting was over, 600 Mexicans were dead and the rest had surrendered. Santa Anna was a prisoner, and the Republic of Texas was free.

This battle—one of the most decisive in history, even though the numbers engaged in it were small—is commemorated by an austere limestone shaft at San Jacinto.

As for San Antonio, the period of its greatest importance in the life of Texas had already passed. When The Alamo fell, San Antonio had 2,500 inhabitants, and was the foremost city in the province. Within fourteen years, even while it was expanding, it had lost its No. 1 rank to Galveston—the Gulf port through which hordes of immigrants now were pouring in, to swell the population of what was first the Republic and then the State of Texas. By 1850, the upstart city of Houston also was beginning to challenge San Antonio.

Not even the Civil War was able to halt the impulsive growth of all three cities. But the postwar era brought a new kind of eminence to San Antonio. It became a cattle center, where herds were assembled for the long drive overland to the railroads in Kansas. The famous Chisholm Trail, with its various offshoots, began in San Antonio. It was to this city that cattle kings and cowhands usually repaired, to celebrate after the drives were over.

San Antonio acquired a notable collection of ornate saloons and sumptuous gambling houses, palatial hotels and restaurants, an Opera House, and other lavish places of entertainment. It became celebrated as a scene of lighthearted frivolity and carefree violence.

The cattle boom ended around 1895, but it had brought a business revival to San Antonio that went on by sheer momentum for another thirty-five years. This change in fortune was helped along in 1900, when a coastal hurricane virtually destroyed San Antonio's arch rival, Galveston. That year San Antonio again became the first city of Texas. It held its position for three decades, through the prosperity of the 1920's. Then, in the morose year 1930, it was overtaken by both Houston and Dallas. It has never regained its prominence as a commercial center.

In Texas today, civic importance depends more on industry than on trade. What industry exists in San Antonio can be separated into three categories, none of them particularly vast or impressive.

There are businesses of local consequence, which have grown with the years. There are oil and cattle companies with home offices in San Antonio, mostly because the proprietors find it an agreeable place to live. And there are a few odd firms, specializing in unusual products, that just happen to make San Antonio their headquarters. One of these, for example, is the Southern Steel Company on South Presa Street. It fabricates cell blocks, artfully designed to forestall escape, for prisons over the nation.

Among the local concerns of some interest nationally are the Pioneer Flour Mills, operated for more than a century by the descendants and successors of a prominent German family, the Guenthers. Another is the Gebhardt Chili Powder Company, which markets a notable brand of Mexican food—chili, beans, tamales, and the fiery condiments that go with them. San Antonio has two of the foremost breweries in the Southwest: the Lone Star Brewing Company and the Pearl Brewing Company. Both maintain handsome grounds and public rooms for convivial meetings.

Most of the oil companies are privately owned. But two at least are public corporations. The Alamo Gas Supply Company was lately formed by Glen A. Martin, one of San Antonio's 150 independent oil

Arneson River Theatre

men, to take over distribution of natural gas in the city. Texstar Corporation, listed on the American Stock Exchange, deals in land, oil, and cattle. Its board of directors includes Tom Slick, a second-generation oilman, who intermittently mounts expeditions to the Himalayas in search of the Abominable Snowman, and who is widely known as the organizer and presiding genius of the Southwest Research Institute.

These random enterprises hardly give San Antonio the busy air of a booming industrial metropolis. In fact, it is often hard for visitors to understand what keeps San Antonio growing—or even going—at all. Unlike New Orleans, it makes no particular effort to preserve its antique flavor. The ladies of the San Antonio Conservation Society fight a continuing rear-guard action to keep its few surviving relics from being cleared away, so that room can be made to park more automobiles.

Yet San Antonio remains the most fascinating—and sometimes the most exasperating—city of Texas. It is perhaps the least characteristically "American" city, not merely in Texas, but in the United States. This quality is due less to the historical fact that San Antonio was for so many years a Spanish-Mexican colonial outpost that to its present cultural affinity with Mexico.

San Antonio is only 150 miles from the Mexican border at Laredo to the south or at Del Rio to the west. It is on the most traveled routes between the United States and Mexico by air, rail, or highway. The part of its population which is of Spanish-Indian stock has been augmented over the years by a steady flow of immigration—much of it unofficial—as well as by birth. It now comes to about 40 per cent of the city's people, who number nearly 600,000 in all.

The Latin section of San Antonio, stretching south and west of the business district, in the same direction from which it came, could be mistaken for a Mexican city. It has its own shops, theaters, cafes, social and business clubs, a weekly newspaper, *La Prensa,* and a Spanish-language television station, KCOR-TV.

Traffic signs are printed in both English and Spanish, as they are on the other side of the border as far south as Monterrey. People of Mexican origin supply most of the clerks in San Antonio's downtown retail establishments—where signs on the windows proclaim *Se habla español*—and most of the gardeners and domestics in the residential areas.

Travel between San Antonio and Mexico is a two-way stream. Cars with Mexican licenses are as common on the streets of San Antonio as windshields with the legend *Turista* on the streets of Mexico City. Besides the immigrants, many well-to-do Mexicans visit the Texas city regularly on business, or simply for amusement. They send their children to be educated in its private schools. They shop in its more expensive stores, where they often keep sizable charge accounts.

Tourists from Mexico (the García-Zuazuas) shop at Frost Bros.

Quincy Howe, Jr.

Quincy How

Street corner

Stairway

Mel Koenning—San Antonio Light

Conversation in a garden

One day recently, for example, René García-Zuazua passed through San Antonio with his wife Francisca and his mother, Sra. Bonnett de Zuazua. They were on their way back to their home in Mexico City, after a trip to New York. The Zuazuas are an old family in Mexico, descended from *conquistadores*. A statue of General Juan Zuazua stands on the Paseo de la Reforma in the capital. Sra. de Zuazua is related to the Kampmanns, an old cattle family in San Antonio. Her son deals in plastic and silk screens.

At Frost Brothers, San Antonio's smart specialty store, the García-Zuazuas shopped for gifts to take home to their three children, and clothes for Francisca. They were personally conducted on their tour by Vice-President Murray Berkowitz. One of the items that pleased them was a $30,000 fur coat made of Russian Barguzin sable. A purchase of that magnitude by a Mexican customer is unusual, but not remarkable at Frost Brothers. Some of their accounts below the border run into five figures, and become complicated when the rate of exchange fluctuates.

Because San Antonio is less opulent than Houston or Dallas, it should not be thought of as a down-at-heels city, living solely on recollections of past splendor. It has plenty of wealthy people left—bankers or absentee oil men or financiers, who make their homes in San Antonio because they like its climate or its atmosphere of leisure and comparative antiquity.

They support a first-rate symphony orchestra, which offers—in addition to the concert season—a two-week opera festival each February, with stars imported from New York. The director of the San Antonio Symphony, Dr. Victor Alessandro, is a native Texan. Born in Waco, the son of a band leader, he studied in Rome, and conducted the Oklahoma Symphony Orchestra for thirteen years before he moved to San Antonio in 1951.

For a Texas city, San Antonio is exceptionally well endowed with private schools. St. Mary's Hall (for girls) and Texas Military Institute (for boys) are both administered by the Episcopal Church, under the eye of the Bishop of West Texas, whose diocesan center is in San Antonio. The Catholic Church supports two excellent colleges for women, Incarnate Word—which draws students from all over the Americas—and Our Lady of the Lake. St. Mary's University, also Catholic, has an outstanding law school.

The most impressive institution architecturally is Trinity University, a protégé of the Presbyterian Church. Created in 1942 by a merger of two smaller colleges (one of them in the town of Waxahachie, near Dal-

44   las), it occupies a handsome modern campus on an eminence above the city. Trinity's bright, clean, functional buildings were designed by a San Antonio architect, O'Neil Ford.

Another architectural feature of San Antonio today is a model housing project for elderly persons. Completed in 1960, with the help of Federal funds, it is a handsome downtown apartment building of nine stories, surrounded by gardens and patios. The furnishings are cunningly designed so that it is nearly impossible for one of the 400 aged tenants, however frail, to fall in the shower, sprain an ankle while bending over to look in the refrigerator, or succumb to loneliness or boredom.

Adorned with sculptures and murals, providing an auditorium, a library, recreation rooms and even a clinic, the Victoria Plaza offers apartments to men and women over sixty-one at an average rent of $27 a month.

As you would expect of a place to which so many people travel, San Antonio is a city of hotels. The largest are the Granada, the Gunter, the Menger, and the St. Anthony. A good deal of the social life of San Antonio goes on in these opulent inns. The San Antonio Club has a decorous suite on the mezzanine of the Gunter. The Alamo Club—which is mostly for entertainment—is off the lobby of the Granada. The St. Anthony provides dinner parties and dancing. As for the Menger, it is the acknowledged headquarters of San Antonio society.

Not only is the Menger an elegant hostelry. It is a historic monument in its own right. Separated from The Alamo by the width of Crockett Street, it shares in some of the glory of that immortal spot. In fact, the Menger once claimed that a cottonwood tree in its patio was the original one for which The Alamo was named. Be that as it may, the Menger is San Antonio's one living link with the bygone era before the Civil War.

It was opened by William A. Menger, as an adjunct to the brewery behind it, on the evening of January 31, 1859. It was not only the largest but the most fashionable resort west of the Mississippi River. Old Sam Houston himself, as governor of Texas, was entertained there. So, at various times, were Robert E. Lee, Phil Sheridan, Theodore Roosevelt, John J. Pershing, Dwight D. Eisenhower, Ulysses S. Grant, Benjamin Harrison, William McKinley, William Howard Taft, Oscar Wilde, William Sidney Porter (O. Henry), and the poet Sidney Lanier.

By World War II, the old Menger had grown rather seedy—though even then the Presidential Suite (No. 102) with its venerable furnishings and its antique wrought-iron balcony, overlooking the Plaza, was a favorite retreat for connoisseurs of nineteenth-century atmosphere. Then it was sold to the National Hotel Company of Galveston. A few years ago they built a handsome addition, extending the Menger all the way around the block by The Alamo, and renovated the rest of it inside, without disturbing its Creole façade. Now, under the polished and adroit management of Ernst V. Kunz, it flourishes again.

Because of its unique situation on Alamo Plaza, the Menger has always been an essential part of every municipal celebration of any consequence. This is particularly true of the Fiesta San Jacinto, the week-long festival that San Antonio puts on each spring, in the seven days that include April 21, the anniversary of the battle.

Mexican woman washes clothes in San Pedro Creek

Mel Koenning—San Antonio Light

46

Mrs. John M. Bennett, Jr., Manager Ernst Kunz, and Mrs. Lewis Moorman, Jr., plan a party at the Menger

The fiesta began as a one-day jubilee back in 1891. Over the years it has burgeoned into a busy calendar of social, patriotic, civic, and commercial ceremonies. It begins with a Pilgrimage to The Alamo by representatives of the participating groups. The pilgrimage is followed by a night Pageant on the River in illuminated barges.

The San Antonio Conservation Society sponsors "A Night in Old San Antonio" at La Villita, where ladies in Spanish costume dispense tacos, chili, and guacamole to hungry—and sedate—revelers. Originally a one-night affair, this folksy gala now lasts the better part of the week. The Coronation of the Queen, in the Municipal Auditorium, is the most extravagant social event.

The climax of the week's entertainment is the Battle of Flowers Parade, a seven-mile procession featuring costly floats decorated with garlands, interspersed with bands, marching units, military vehicles, and riders on horseback, winding over a route that ends before a bank of reviewing stands facing The Alamo.

The final event is the Saturday night Fiesta Flambeau Parade. It honors Miss Fiesta, who is chosen by the businessmen's Fiesta San Jacinto Association.

In between these spectacles are exhibitions of art, flowers, costumes, and acrobatic skill; balls, receptions, military reviews, street dancing, fashion shows, dinner meetings, and memorial services, by organizations which include the Texas Pioneers, the Daughters and Wives of the Old Trail Drivers of Texas, the Order of The Alamo, the Texas Cavaliers, the San Antonio Charro Association, and the South Texas Press Association. Guests usually include, besides the city officials, the Governor of Texas, a congressman or two, and the commanders of San Antonio's military installations.

The military commanders are important. A good deal of the fiesta's abundance is due to their generous policy of joining in community projects. Not only do they enter lavish floats, bands, and marching units in the parades, also they supply many of the flat-bed trucks and trailers on which other floats are built, provide lumber and carpenters for the reviewing stands, furnish military police to guard the spectators, medical attendants and ambulances to care for them in case of emergency, cameramen with lights and film and equipment to record the extravaganza. Without this contribution by the armed forces, the fiesta would be a modest provincial holiday.

For the fact is that San Antonio has come back to the circumstances

Grounds of the Lone Star Brewing Company

Quincy Howe, Jr.

of its origin, when it was primarily a Spanish garrison town. Since World War I, while it has fallen behind Houston and Dallas as an industrial center, San Antonio has acquired a new distinction as the home of what is probably the largest military establishment in America. It includes a major Army post and four important Air Force bases.

Fort Sam Houston, covering more than five square miles inside the city, is the headquarters of the Fourth Army administrative area, reaching from Louisiana to New Mexico. Also at Fort Sam is Brooke Army Medical Center, with a 2,000-bed hospital, research laboratories, and the Army's basic school for medical officers, nurses, and technicians.

Kelly Air Force Base, founded as a flight school in 1917, now is a huge aircraft maintenance and supply depot, with 24,000 civilian employees, acres of shops and warehouses, miles of concrete runways, railroad spurs, and sidings. Comparable in size to a steel corporation or a division of General Motors, Kelly is San Antonio's only large industrial operation, and the financial base of its prosperity.

Lackland Air Force Base, next door to Kelly, is the principal Air Force training school for recruits and officer candidates. Randolph Air Force Base, northeast of the city, was known to a generation of flying cadets as "The West Point of the Air." It is now the executive headquarters of the far-reaching Air Training Command.

San Antonio has a hand in the space age, too. At Brooks Air Force Base, near Kelly and Lackland, is the brand-new $10,000,000 plant of the Aerospace Medical Center, which also operates the model 1,000-bed Air Force hospital at Lackland. The center trains flight surgeons and conducts medical research on conditions in space.

These military activities largely account for the fabulous growth of San Antonio between 1940 and 1960, when—without any private industry of great significance—it leaped from thirty-sixth to seventeenth place among the populous cities of the country. They also explain its abiding attraction for retired members of the armed services, who permeate its social, business, and professional life.

In San Antonio, the one-time soldier or airman can add to his retirement pay by taking a job in which he deals with old acquaintances who are still in uniform. For entertainment, he joins his former comrades at the spacious Fort Sam—or Randolph—Officers' Club. If he falls sick, he is treated by top-flight specialists at Brooke Army Hospital or the Aerospace Medical Center. And when the bugle blows taps for him the last time, he can—if he wishes—receive a military funeral at the Fort Sam Houston National Cemetery.

3: The Hill Country

View from the Flying L Ranch

O N the outskirts of San Antonio, to the west, the land rises on the first of two great natural terraces, climbing toward the High Plains in the Panhandle. Known as the Balcones Fault, this wide escarpment starts in Del Rio, on the Rio Grande, swings around to the east, by San Antonio, and then northward in the direction of Fort Worth.

The rise is gentle; at first you hardly notice it. From about 700 feet above sea level by The Alamo, you mount through broken hills, until you stand on the vast table of the Edwards Plateau, 2,000 feet high, in West Texas.

The rocky slope, garnished with tassels of crooked mesquite and feathery huisache, is called the Hill Country. It is a haunt of wild life— deer and jack rabbits, armadillos, beavers, wild turkeys, and doves—and is one of the playgrounds of Texas.

Here begin the dude ranches that give a temperate taste of western living to the visitor from the East. Within fifty miles of San Antonio are at least a dozen guest ranches, large and small, festive or quiet, providing horses, usually a swimming pool, real or synthetic cowhands, campfire parties, and square dancing. Two of the best are the Mission Valley, near New Braunfels, a few miles north of the city, and the Gallegher Ranch at Helotes, a few miles to the west.

Beyond Helotes, in the foothills, is the town of Bandera, a whole community dedicated to the vocation of entertaining visitors, western style. Bandera goes in for dance halls with old-time country fiddlers, for rodeos, and frontier celebrations. It has the largest concentration of guest ranches in Texas.

One of the most comfortable—and certainly the most unusual—is the Flying L Ranch, a couple of miles out of Bandera. Actually, the Flying L is a ranch in atmosphere only. What it really is might be defined as a motel for the air age. Like nearly all the larger guest ranches now-adays, the Flying L has its own airstrip for private flyers. The difference is that the Flying L caters primarily to airline pilots and stewardesses on vacation, to week-end meetings of business executives who arrive in company airplanes, and to the growing fellowship of ordinary citizens who travel on their own wings.

The Flying L was the creation of the late Colonel Jack Lapham, a long-time director of Texaco—and the son of one of its founders—who

Rancher Bernard Petty feeds Suffolk sheep

was besides an expert polo player and a pilot. It was an outgrowth of an elementary flight school which he had operated for the Air Force in San Antonio during World War II. Still flying regularly in his sixties, Colonel Lapham died in a crash at the Flying L a few years ago, as he was coming in for a landing on the strip.

The Ranch is now the property of his widow, Lucy Jane Lapham—who would fly with the Colonel in the old days as his copilot—and is managed by his former assistant, Mark A. Chism. It offers all the luxuries that other guest ranches provide, including suites of air-conditioned rooms with fireplaces and private verandas, and also a hangar in which to park your airplane.

A little north of Bandera, the main highway to West Texas from San Antonio mounts into the hills, through the pleasant old German towns of Boerne and Comfort. Kerrville, on the Guadalupe River beyond them,

The Hill Country

is a center for summer camps, summer homes, hunting lodges, and health institutions. It is also something of a religious center.

Most of the church denominations of Texas, and many other youth-building organizations, operate camps for boys and girls in the Hill Country around Kerrville. They include a Boy Scout camp which was once the ranch of Eastern Airlines President Eddie Rickenbacker; a Y.M.C.A. Camp; camps for Catholic, Episcopal, Methodist, and Presbyterian young people; and the Texas Lions Camp for Crippled Children.

Near Mountain Home, a few miles above Kerrville, is an open tabernacle on a hilltop, overlooking a grove of trees. It is the site of the interdenominational Hill Country Camp Meeting, inaugurated by the late Dr. Pierre Bernard Hill of San Antonio. For eight days in August each year, it draws as many as 3,000 summer folks and ranch dwellers around the countryside into the shade of the tabernacle for old-fashioned preaching, while their wives and daughters prepare barbecue and salad, pie and coffee, under the trees below.

The dry air and sunshine around Kerrville make it a health resort. Besides the big U. S. Veterans' Hospital at Legion, outside the city, there are two state hospitals, the modern Kerrville General Hospital, two private hospitals, and a Home for the Aged. Schreiner Institute, a handsome junior college under the auspices of the Presbyterian Church, is named for the dominant banking and commercial family of Kerrville.

Along the Guadalupe above Kerrville—especially between Ingram

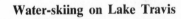
Water-skiing on Lake Travis

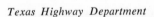
Texas Highway Department

54 and Hunt, where the river has been dammed to form a pair of small lakes —are rows of inconspicuous but eminently comfortable summer homes, usually with boat landings on the water. They belong to the families of affluent oil men and industrialists, who live as far away as Houston or Beaumont.

The same provident men pay substantial sums for hunting leases on ranches throughout the Hill Country. A frequent sight, on crisp nights in the fall, is a succession of Cadillacs heading back toward Houston, each with a spread of antlers draped on both front fenders.

In 1952—the last year for which figures are available—hunters in Kerr County killed 3,800 deer, a record for the season in Texas. Almost as many were taken in Llano and Gillespie Counties, to the north. Altogether, more than 100,000 deer are killed each year in Texas, a large proportion of them in the Hill Country.

There is no danger that the area will be depopulated. Deer thrive on the wooded slopes, in such numbers that they even wander down into cities like San Antonio and Austin, to get themselves hung up in fences around suburban homes. Hill Country ranchers consider them a nuisance, because they browse on the leafy branches of the same stunted oaks and mesquite trees as the goats.

Angora goats are the prime economic resource of the Hill Country. They are descended from Angora rams brought to the United States from Turkey more than a century ago, and bred to ordinary milk goats in this country. Colonel William W. Haupt introduced them into Texas, and they quickly spread over the flanks of the Balcones Escarpment.

By 1940 there were 3,300,000 Angora goats in Texas—more than in any other part of the world, including Angora. An eight-year drought, beginning in 1949, dried up the streams, caused the trees to wither, and cut the Angora population in Texas by almost one-half. But the rains returned in the spring of 1957. Soon there were nearly as many Angoras as there had been before.

The goats produce a long, lustrous coat, which is made into a fabric known as mohair. Both durable and rich in texture, it was once used widely to cover chairs and automobile seats, as well as in drapes and clothing. In recent years, it has been largely replaced by mixtures of wool and cotton, or by synthetic fibers. Yet mohair even now is worth a good deal of money to ranchers in the Hill Country.

The biggest of the goat ranchers for a good many years were the Stielers, who lived between Comfort and Fredericksburg, a few miles out of Kerrville. Adolf Stieler and his brother, the late Fritz Stieler, were grandsons of a German immigrant who settled in Kerrville in 1854. Their father married a Schreiner, of the prosperous Kerrville family, and moved out into the hills to raise goats.

At one time, Adolf Stieler—a big, hospitable man, with a broad Teutonic accent—kept around 37,000 Angoras. In recent years, he has reduced his herd to about one-fifth its former size, adding a few thousand sheep and some cattle. He owns about 150 square miles of the Hill Country, and leases thirty more. A kind-hearted herdsman who hates to shoot animals, Adolf Stieler feeds corn to the deer that congregate around his home.

Adolf Stieler with goats

Art Kowert

Adolf's son Eugene (known as "Duro") prefers cattle. He lives with his wife and daughter on a big ranch at Sierra Blanca, far out in West Texas, which he owns jointly with his father. Adolf's daughter Helen ("Schatzy") married a classmate at the University of Texas, John ("Hondo") Crouch. They live with their four children on a ranch about five miles from Adolf's on the way to Fredericksburg. Hondo also is a partner with Adolf in a wool-and-mohair warehouse at Comfort.

A good many of the notable names around San Antonio and the Hill Country are German in origin, like Adolf Stieler's. This is by no means a coincidence. The Anglo-American farmers who followed Stephen F. Austin to Texas after 1821 were in turn followed by an influx of German settlers, beginning in 1845.

Their leader was a hardy and resourceful young aristocrat from Hesse, Prince Karl zu Solms-Braunfels, representing a group of German noblemen who sponsored the emigration. Their object was the same one that had brought their predecessors to America: economic and political freedom.

Prince Karl, with four companions, arrived in San Antonio in July 1844. He arranged with Captain John Coffee Hays of the Texas Rangers to survey a sizable tract of land which could be bought from the Republic. Then he headed for the Gulf Coast, to find a suitable port for the first shipload of colonists, who were already on their way.

Near the entrance to Matagorda Bay, he founded the port of Karlshafen—later known as Indianola, the busiest port in Texas until a hurricane wiped it off the map, forty-two years afterward. At Karlshafen, in the next few months, more than 6,000 Germans landed.

Prince Karl in person led the first contingent up to the Hill Country, over a trail on which he was planning to lay a wooden track for horse-drawn cars, until a railroad could be built. At the meeting of the Guadalupe and Comal Rivers, in the wilderness between San Antonio and the half-deserted capital at Austin, he settled them on 1,265 acres which he acquired—for a little more than $1,000—in the name of the Mainzer Adelsverein, the Emigration Society of Mainz, Germany. The town he built there was called New Braunfels, after the village in which Prince Karl had been born. Another township, a mile or two away, is known as Solms.

The attraction of New Braunfels was much the same as the one which had led to the founding of San Antonio, a century and a quarter earlier. Bubbling up out of many clear springs, only three miles from the Guadalupe, was the limpid Comal River, which draws something over

200 million gallons daily from the limestone reservoirs underneath the Hill Country.

It was named by the Spaniards for the innumerable small islands in it—some only a yard or so across—resembling earthenware pans, or *comales,* on a stove. The city was laid out on neatly ordered squares, with solid houses surrounded by graveled yards, in the archaic style of Northern Europe. Prince Karl built his own castle, Schloss Sophienburg, on an eminence above the town. It is now a museum.

From New Braunfels the German colonists spread over the Hill Country. Their strongest outpost is Fredericksburg, fifty-five miles northwest of New Braunfels, where Adolf Stieler goes to consort with his ranching friends.

It would be hard to find an enterprise in Fredericksburg with anything except a German name. The favorite resting place for tourists passing through that pastoral town is the Nimitz Hotel, founded by the family of Fleet Admiral Chester W. Nimitz, World War II commander of the United States Pacific Fleet, who is now retired in California.

But New Braunfels is the acknowledged capital of the German community in Texas. The weekly New Braunfelser *Zeitung*—now the *Zeitung-Chronicle*—has been recording their activities without interruption since November 1852. Its first editor was Ferdinand Jacob Lindheimer, known as "the father of Texas botany." Today it is edited by Frederic Oheim, descendant of another early settler.

The official historian of Comal County is Oscar Haas, grandson of a New Braunfels founder, who also is county treasurer. Several of the city's businesses have been handed down from the days of Prince Karl.

Another old German institution that flourishes in New Braunfels and the Hill Country is the *Sängerverein,* or Singing Society. The first German singers' club was organized at New Braunfels in 1850, and held its initial *Sängerfest* on July 4, 1853, in a makeshift *Sängerhalle* beside the Guadalupe.

The Texanischer Gebirgs-Sängerbund, consisting of societies around the state, meets annually in one or another Germanic city for a weekend of choral singing and *Gemütlichkeit.* Between festivals, New Braunfels citizens drink lager and sing German songs—when the *Kinder* aren't playing cow-cow boogie on the jukebox—at Hans Schwamkrug's rustic beer garden.

Comal Springs, at the head of the river, has been converted into Landa Park, one of the loveliest recreation spots in Texas. Named for another pioneer German family, it includes an enormous fresh-water

58

Quincy Howe, Jr.

German Pioneer Memorial at Fredericksburg

Comal Treasurer Oscar Haas reads the paper

swimming pool, created by damming a part of the Comal River bed. Private homes line the river, farther on toward the Guadalupe.

Many of the little islands that gave the river its name have been circled by retaining walls or linked with the shore by footbridges. They are used for boat landings or picnic grounds or places where swimmers can sit and meditate, with their feet trailing in the water.

Besides all of these attractions, New Braunfels is blessed with flour mills and plants producing cotton goods, hosiery, cedar oil, tanned leather, and German sausages.

The Hill Country is richly endowed with odd and interesting places. Only seventeen miles from New Braunfels, on the way to Austin, is the town of San Marcos. It is a county seat with a few modest industries, and is the home of Southwest Texas State College for teachers.

Here is another collection of prolific springs, pouring their freshets into the San Marcos River. Here too the river has been dammed, to form Spring Lake; and a concession on Spring Lake operates the Aquarena Submarine Theatre.

The auditorium is an excursion boat with a glass bottom, through which the audience peers down into the lake. In the iridescent gloom below, pretty girl skin divers with frogmen's feet perform stately dances, or go through the motions of eating lunch.

Any spectacle involving considerable amounts of water is fascinating to Texans, because so much of Texas is so dry. Despite its profusion of springs and cypress-bordered rivers, the Hill Country is no exception. Its average rainfall is about thirty inches a year, dropping off on the plateau above to about eight inches at El Paso.

Most of the rain it does get comes down in torrential storms or sudden cloudbursts. A large part of it rolls away to the Gulf; the rest filters down into the underground rock, leaving the hills dry again. In a land that is generally dun-colored, with an insubstantial film of dust on its foliage, lakes and streams have a particular enchantment.

This part of Texas is the home of Lyndon Johnson. He was born near Johnson City, a Hill Country town which his grandfather founded, between Fredericksburg and Austin. He attended Southwest Texas State College in San Marcos.

As a young congressman, his proudest achievement was the building of a series of dams along the Colorado River, above Austin, that brought rural electrification to the ranchers in the hills. Now he lives on a 200-acre ranch of his own at Stonewall, beside the Pedernales River, between Johnson City and Fredericksburg.

Pedernales (pronounced "Pertinallis" by folks who live along the river) is from a Spanish word meaning "flint." In the sense that he strikes fire by his contact with others, the word describes Lyndon Johnson. Gregarious like the late President Roosevelt, whom he admired and resembles, Johnson has the same faculty of inciting the company around him to action.

The LBJ Ranch is as accustomed to state visitors as Hyde Park was, though not on quite the same Olympian scale. Among the chief executives who have been guests there are President John F. Kennedy, Chancellor Konrad Adenauer of Germany, and President Adolfo López Mateos of Mexico. A retinue of aides accompanies the owner when he is in residence at the ranch. He maintains a permanent office staff in Austin as well as in Washington, and is in constant communication with both by telephone.

The means to conduct his affairs in this open-handed manner—which is modest enough by Texas standards—have been provided largely through the business acumen of the Vice-President's wife, Lady Bird. Mrs. Johnson, who was Claudia Taylor from East Texas, came into a small fortune from her mother's family soon after she was married, and invested part of it in an Austin radio station.

By her native shrewdness—and no doubt with some help from people who hoped to gain her husband's favor—Mrs. Johnson has built this investment into a million-dollar corporation, the LBJ Company, with TV stations in Austin and Weslaco, real estate, an interest in a bank, and other properties.

They earn enough to make the Johnsons and their family (they have two daughters, Lynda Bird and Lucy Baines Johnson) financially independent. The Vice-President relies on his virtuosity in guiding the whims of a volatile electorate—but not for a living. Rather, he relies on it as a source of power for the political activity which his finely tempered nerves demand.

Since his elevation to the Vice-Presidency—if it can be considered an elevation—Lyndon Johnson's neighbors have been wondering whether the same thing will happen to him that happened to one of his predecessors from Texas, John Nance Garner. When the New Deal had stretched his Texas-bred conservatism as far as it would reach, Garner found that he was no longer welcome at the White House, and was then summarily retired to his home in Uvalde.

Johnson is much more adaptable than Garner was, and a good deal more liberal in his outlook. But he has been used to running his own

Vice-President and Lady Bird ford the Pedernales

office on his own authority, exercising a power independent of the President's, though responsive to it. Many admirers of Lyndon Johnson, when they voted against him for the Vice-Presidency in 1960, did so because they felt that—whichever way his relationship with the President worked out—his usefulness to Texas was at an end.

As these observers saw it, if he subordinated himself to the Chief Executive, he would become simply a handy man, doing odd jobs at the Capitol. But if he tried to follow his own instinct for individual action, he would find that the President is the man in whom the only real executive authority is vested. In either case, Texas would have lost a national leader in the Senate—and Lyndon Johnson's brilliant career would be finished.

Quincy Howe, Jr.

Tom Miller Dam on the Colorado at Austin

Be that as it may, so far the State of Texas has responded like a spirited horse to his guidance. For those who see a land of promise on the New Frontier, he represents it. For those who view the prospect with dismay, he is all that stands between them and the crack of doom. Either way, Texans have been proceeding on the assumption that Johnson is a Texan first, and the President's elongated shadow only second.

The visible monuments to Lyndon Johnson, in his own countryside, include a network of electric power lines and transformers, striding over the bare hills. Among the places to which they have given light is the state-owned Longhorn Cavern, near the town of Burnet. Still not fully explored, it is said to be the third largest cave system in the nation, after the Carlsbad Caverns of New Mexico and the Mammoth Cave in Kentucky.

Electricity has brought to the Longhorn Cavern a concession operating a six-mile tour through its underground chambers, with rest rooms and refreshments at intervals. There is also a camp site outside.

Even more impressive than the cavern is the string of artificial lakes behind the dams that furnish its power. Although they were built solely for utilitarian reasons, they have turned the Hill Country between Burnet and Austin into a handsome inland-lake area, for the pleasure of its citizens and visitors. There are six of these Highland Lakes, winding along the Colorado River, from a point about sixty miles northwest of Austin into the outskirts of the city.

The highest of them is Lake Buchanan, in a comparatively wild region midway between Burnet and Llano. It also has the widest sweep of open water—about four by eight miles on the main body of the lake—although it is only half the size of Lake Travis in its total volume. Much of the shore of Lake Buchanan is still remote and deserted, untouched by highways.

Three smaller lakes descend from it, down the river, leading into the vast reach of Lake Travis, at the junction of the Colorado and the Pedernales. Lake Travis rambles through the hills for a distance of sixty-five miles, and ranges up to about two miles in width at its broadest point, behind Mansfield Dam. With 270 miles of shore, bordered by woods and brush, it provides some of the best fishing for bass anywhere in the Southwest.

Lake Travis has become a paradise for landlocked sailors. Some 25,000 small craft ply its waters, varying in size and luxury from skiffs up to fifty-foot cabin cruisers. The new town of Lago Vista—developed by Dr. C. Paul Harris, a Houston dentist—has grown up to shelter the owners and to service their boats.

George Seagert

Lake Austin from Mount Bonnell

Lago Vista is a neat collection of modern, California-style homes for well-to-do vacationers and retired folk. It has a paved airstrip, a swimming pool, docks, and piers for fishermen. Just outside the town is the Bar K Guest Ranch, with another paved airstrip. Around a couple of bends in the lake, on the opposite shore, is a lavish resort for motorists who trail their boats behind them, the Lake Travis Lodges.

Lake Austin, the last of the six, is really a suburban extension of the capital city of Texas. Its center of activity is Lake Austin Park, a municipal recreation spot, twelve miles from the city limits. Farther on, around the devious shore, is the county-owned Quinlan Park.

A stern-wheel excursion boat, the *Commodore Perry,* plies the twenty-two-mile length of Lake Austin from Tom Miller Dam, on the western edge of Austin, to the foot of Mansfield Dam, where Lake Travis begins. Some 4,000 private craft are registered on Lake Austin. The residential area of the city is moving out in that direction.

Austin was the fourth or fifth capital of Texas, after the Republic declared its independence in March 1836. At Washington-on-the-Brazos, where the provisional government met, President David G. Burnet chose the town of Harrisburg (long since swallowed up by Houston) as the temporary capital. Before any business of importance could be transacted, the approach of Mexican General Santa Anna drove the President and his Cabinet off to a haven on Galveston Island.

After Santa Anna surrendered, they spent several months in Columbia, a few miles down the coast. Then they moved back to Houston, which had been established at the head of navigation on Buffalo Bayou, close to Harrisburg.

In 1839 the new President, Mirabeau B. Lamar, appointed a commission of five members to go look for another capital, less rowdy than Houston and in a more central location. They picked the isolated village of Waterloo, on the north bank of the Colorado.

The Congress of Texas confirmed their selection on January 19, 1840. Its name was changed to Austin, in honor of the man who had brought the first Anglo-American settlers into the country, only eighteen years earlier. A group of log houses in the new capital served as the seat of government until they could erect a more nearly permanent home.

For the first half-century of its existence, Austin was a somewhat smaller, more provincial copy of San Antonio. Like the old Spanish capital, seventy-five miles to the south and west, it was a cattle town with muddy streets, a few fine homes (including the stately Governor's Mansion, put up in 1856), and a goodly number of gaudy saloons and gam-

The State Capitol at Austin

Quincy Howe, Jr.

Administration Tower, University of Texas

cy Howe, Jr.

University Christian Church in Austin

bling palaces. O. Henry lived there for a while, and started writing stories to augment his meager salary as a bank clerk. Other notable residents— of a nonpolitical cast—included Elizabet Ney, the sculptor, and her husband, Dr. Edmund D. Montgomery.

The great, domed Capitol of pink granite—bigger than the nation's Capitol in Washington—began as a real-estate promotion in 1881. The state government traded off three million acres of empty land in the Panhandle to a syndicate of Chicago builders, at $1 an acre, in return for a $3,000,000 Capitol. The cornerstone was laid in March 1885, and the building was formally opened three years later. The flesh-colored stone for its walls was quarried from Granite Mountain in the Hill Country near Marble Falls.

The University of Texas, founded on a land grant of two million acres in 1883, benefited by its endowment in a different way. Prohibited by law from selling the land, it struck oil and leased the drilling rights instead. As of June 1960, the university had salted away nearly $357,-000,000 from its domain, to become the richest educational institution in the United States, and possibly in the world. Besides a vast plant with 18,000 students in Austin, it includes medical branches in Galveston, Houston, and Dallas, and also Texas Western College in El Paso.

As Texas and its wealth have grown since 1890, so has Austin, the seat of its government. In addition to the permanent state agencies that make the city their headquarters, it houses members of the Legislature

World War II Memorial, Austin

Quincy Howe, Jr.

when they come to town, along with the open-handed lobbyists who follow them; Federal offices, such as that of the District Director of Internal Revenue; some 160 state-wide associations with an interest in what happens at the capital; and the news correspondents and wire service representatives who cover all these official and semi-official activities.

Austin, like San Antonio, has some excellent hotels. Among them are the Stephen F. Austin, the old Driskill, and the Commodore Perry. (Visitors attuned to the nuances of international intrigue are startled sometimes, when they pick up bright red match books at the Commodore Perry, bearing the initials *CP*.)

A number of historic sites remain in Austin from the days of the Republic. One is a colonial mansion with the legend above its entrance, "Légation de France." It was built in 1840 for Count Alphonse de Savigny, Minister to Texas from King Louis Philippe.

Austin has little of the frontier flavor that permeates the Hill Country. From the beginning, it has been a home of politicians, administrators, and of course scholars. A certain sophistication—characteristic of professional men and civil servants—marks the atmosphere of Austin.

Yet it looks to the west, on the serpentine lakes which have filled up the valley of the Colorado. In that direction is the man whose presence is most felt in Austin today. As the era of Sam Houston fades into antiquity, the era of Lyndon Johnson has grown increasingly distinct. The source from which Austin now derives its strength is not the musty Capitol, but a ranch on the Pedernales.

4: *Pioneer Land:*
East Texas

The Guadalupe River near Gonzales

Hartwell J. Kennard, Jr.

PEOPLE with an inquisitive turn of mind, traveling through the prosperous countryside of East Texas, sometimes ask, "How does it happen that Anglo-American settlers have succeeded so well in this region, where the Spaniards failed?"

Obviously it doesn't do to answer that the Anglo-Americans were hardier, or better colonizers, or more experienced in exploiting a new land. For the Spaniards were eminently successful in Mexico—and in fact throughout America south of the Rio Grande—where conditions were less favorable to agriculture or trade than in Texas, and the Indians who occupied those places first were more troublesome.

One reason the Spaniards failed in East Texas is that they weren't so much interested in settling there as they were in keeping the French out.

Roadside park outside of Nacogdoches

Texas Highway Department

Texas Highway Department

Monument to soldiers of the Texas Republic near La Grange

They were content to establish a few frontier posts around Nacogdoches, near the Louisiana border, where they could watch for any encroachment on their territory. Even these lasted only a few years, and hardly any trace of them remains today.

The most enduring garrison wasn't actually in Texas at all. It was the Presidio of Nuestra Señora del Pilar de los Adaes, near what is now the town of Robeline, Louisiana. Los Adaes was the Spanish capital of Texas for fifty years, until the provincial government was transferred to San Antonio in 1772. It was responsible for the introduction of a considerable Spanish influence into Louisiana—but it left no permanent mark on the culture of Texas.

A more fundamental reason for the failure of the Spaniards in East Texas might be found in the fact that these bayous, trailing festoons of so-called Spanish moss, these forests of pine and hickory, these undulating prairies of rich black soil, called up in their minds no recollection of Spain. They were at home on the bare mountain slopes and in the narrow valleys of Mexico, or even on the vast, arid plateau of West Texas. But this was to them an alien land, made for agriculture on a grand scale, such as they had never known in Spain.

It was exactly what the Anglo-American pioneers wanted. When they came pouring in after 1821, out of Tennessee and Alabama, in response to Stephen Austin's call, they followed the same route which the Spaniards had laid out, across the Sabine River, through Nacogdoches. But few of them went on to San Antonio and the west. Instead, they settled on the broad, empty meadows between the Brazos and the Colorado Rivers, roughly halfway across the plain to San Antonio from Louisiana. There they started putting up log houses and planting grain in the fertile fields around them. East Texas, as they saw it before their dazzled eyes, was a wide expanse of virgin ground, waiting for the plow.

The first towns were Columbus, on the Colorado eighty miles southeast of what was later to become Austin, and Washington-on-the-Brazos, fifty miles northeast of the settlement at Columbus. This is the part of Texas through which most of the rivers pass, growing broader and deeper as they roll toward the Gulf. Besides the Brazos and the Colorado, they include the Guadalupe, coming down out of the Hill Country, the Trinity, the Neches, and the Sabine itself, besides such lesser streams or tributaries as the Navidad, the San Bernard, or the Navasota.

It was at Washington-on-the-Brazos, in a small frame house, that the Declaration of Texas Independence was signed in 1836. A replica of the house now stands in Washington State Park, between the towns of Navasota and Brenham.

From these centers the early civilization of Texas spread over the prairie in all directions, avoiding the dry plateau to the west until after the Civil War. It was an agrarian culture, derived from the plantation life of the states from which the pioneers had come—but with certain differences. There were no great numbers of slaves in East Texas. These settlers mostly were farmers, who prospered by their own strength and ingenuity. The homes they built—like the old Cavitt House at Wheelock, now the property of Holland McCombs—were modified colonial mansions, suitable to the frontier. Like the lives of their owners, they were comfortably substantial, but not pretentious.

It was precisely because this countryside was home to the Anglo-American settlers—whereas it was only a strategic territory to the government below the Rio Grande—that they were able to resist the

Mementoes of George Sessions Perry in his home at Rockdale

Mexicans who succeeded to the rule of Spain. The defeat of Santa Anna did not end Mexico's effort to retrieve the lost province. In 1842, Mexican armies twice invaded Texas, capturing San Antonio and several other towns before they retired across the border.

At La Grange, on the Colorado a few miles above Columbus, is a monument to thirty-three settlers under Captain Nicholas Mosby Dawson, who were surrounded and killed in an attempt to relieve San Antonio the second time it was taken. The same monument commemorates the death of seventeen men who were executed in Mexico, after the failure of an attack on the Mexican border town of Mier.

This part of Texas was the home of the late George Sessions Perry, who wrote with more warmth and humor about the descendants of these pioneers than any other Texas author in recent years. Although Perry was best known, toward the end of his comparatively short life, for descriptive books like *Texas: A World in Itself* and magazine articles in the *Saturday Evening Post,* his early novels and stories—*Walls Rise Up, Hold Autumn in Your Hand, Hackberry Cavalier*—were filled with vivid scenes of boys and vagabonds catfishing in the Brazos, sharecroppers picking cotton, and Negroes hoeing Johnson grass.

The first settlers in this section had planted grain and garden crops, kept some stock, and prospered. Their grandchildren turned to cotton, because it brought a quick return in cash—and for a while they prospered too.

But cotton wears the land out, unless it is constantly enriched with plant foods and chemicals. By the time George Perry was a grown man in Rockdale, near the San Gabriel River, which flows into the Brazos, cotton and the long drought of the early 1930's had left this area of East Texas an exhausted country.

One of the things that Perry did for Rockdale—after he made some money writing about it for magazines in the East—was to show the farmers around it how they could get back on their feet again by raising cattle. Now, you might assume that this would be an obvious idea to anybody in Texas, where people are popularly supposed to be born wearing cowboy boots. But cattle ranching was inherited from the Spaniards, who introduced it into the brush country of South Texas; and later on it spread over the dry plains to the west, where nothing much would grow except grass. Rockdale was in East Texas—and East Texas was a land of overalls and lumber jackets, not blue jeans or leather chaps.

George Perry took over a tired stretch of pasture outside of Rockdale, stocked it with beef steers, and turned it into a ranch. Before long the farmers around the countryside were competing in rodeos and holding cattle auctions every week. Milam County now has more than 50,000 head of cattle, ranking with some of the ranch preserves in West Texas and the Panhandle. Over the thirty years that ended in 1956, its cotton harvest dropped from nearly 70,000 bales to a little more than 10,000. The same trend has been at work in most of the agricultural sections of East Texas, converting it from an outpost of the Old South to an integral part of the West.

Rockdale is representative of East Texas in another respect. Milam County sits on a big vein of lignite, which is a kind of brownish product of decayed vegetation, midway between peat and coal. In the early days it was mined in a desultory way for fuel, before the discovery in Texas of vast underground pools of oil and natural gas.

A few years ago, the Aluminum Company of America, looking around for a cheap source to supply the enormous quantities of electric power needed in smelting aluminum, happened on the idle lignite mine outside of Rockdale.

Now Rockdale has a $100,000,000 Alcoa plant, producing 150,000 tons of aluminum a year. It is the largest of three Texas aluminum smelters (the others are on the Gulf Coast near Corpus Christi and Port Lavaca) that make the Lone Star State a major producer of that shining metal, though it has no bauxite ore of its own. Also, the Alcoa plant at Rockdale provides a neat example of the way in which Texas has diversified its economy, combining pastoral pursuits with industry on the same wide and reputedly lonesome prairie.

The same contrast between the agrarian culture of pioneer times and the increasingly modern technology of today can be seen—in one form or another—throughout East Texas. A few miles to the east of Rockdale, on the other side of the Brazos, is the city of Bryan. It is the seat of Brazos County, one of the earliest Anglo-American communities. It is

es Taylor

Aluminum workers at Rockdale's Alcoa plant

Roland Chatham

Brazos County Courthouse at Bryan

also the site of Bryan Air Force Base, a major air-age center for the training of jet pilots.

To administer the county's business, Bryan has put up a courthouse which is as far removed as possible from the sandstone-and-marble mausoleums that brood over most county seats in Texas. Looking more like a smart shopping center, it cost $1,000,000 and has won a number of national awards for architectural design.

Bryan's influence extends far beyond Brazos County, through a self-contained activity just beyond the city limits. At suburban College Station is the Agricultural and Mechanical College of Texas—better known as Texas A&M, an institution of much more prestige and importance than its rather prosaic name suggests.

In the first place, A&M ranks with the university at Austin as a state educational system, and has its own land-grant funds. Also it is an experimental laboratory for advanced research in agricultural methods, plant biology, animal husbandry, conservation, and pest control. A&M administers the organization of county agricultural agents, who pass on the results of its research to farmers around the state; and also the Texas Forest Service.

In addition to all that, it is one of the top military academies in the United States. In both World Wars, Texas A&M contributed more officers to the Army, Navy, and Air Force than either West Point or Annapolis. Its graduates include such notable military men as the nation's foremost expert on ballistic missiles, Lieutenant General Bernard A. Schriever,

Old Austin Hall at Sam Houston State College, Huntsville

head of the Air Research and Development Command of the Air Force, whose home is in San Antonio.

And finally—like the university—A&M includes in its system a collection of satellite schools that teach agricultural techniques. These are Tarleton State College at Stephenville, southwest of Fort Worth; Arlington State College, beween Fort Worth and Dallas; and Prairie View A&M College for Negroes, near Hempstead, in the direction of Houston.

It would be impossible in a book of this kind and scope to show all the facilities for higher education in Texas, with their distinctive atmospheres and traditions. Scattered over the state are no less than fifty-nine colleges and universities—not counting theological seminaries, business schools, academies of one sort or another, junior colleges, or medical branches of other institutions.

Apart from the two big state systems, the most renowned seats of learning are privately owned by the dominant church organizations of Texas. Among them are Baylor University (Baptist) at Waco, Southern Methodist University in Dallas, and Texas Christian University in Fort Worth.

The foremost technical university of Texas is the nonsectarian Rice University in Houston. A city-owned institution of increasing note is the University of Houston. Some of the smaller schools enjoy considerable eminence. They include Austin College in Sherman, Hardin-Simmons University in Abilene, Southwestern University in Georgetown, and Texas Wesleyan College in Fort Worth.

In the same category is a third group of state colleges which are not attached either to the university or to A&M. They are Lamar State College of Technology in Beaumont, North Texas State College in Denton, Texas College of Arts and Industries at Kingsville, Texas Southern University for Negroes in Houston, Texas Technological College in Lubbock, and Texas Women's University in Denton.

By no means last in service to their own communities are the colleges that belong to a fourth large group of state-owned institutions. They started out as training schools for teachers, but in most cases have grown into regional academies of arts and sciences as well. They include East Texas State College at Commerce, Sam Houston State College at Huntsville, Southwest Texas State College at San Marcos, Stephen F. Austin State College at Nacogdoches, Sul Ross State College at Alpine—beyond the Pecos—and West Texas State College at Canyon, in the Panhandle.

All but the last two of these are east of the Balcones Escarpment. That's for the obvious reason that higher education started in the older communities of East Texas.

Sam Houston State College, for example, is at Huntsville, fifty miles east of Bryan, in the wooded area of Texas as you approach Louisiana. Huntsville is where Sam Houston spent the last years of his life, after serving twice as President of the Republic, fourteen years as a senator from Texas, and briefly as governor on the eve of the Civil War.

The plain white "Steamboat House" in which Houston died at the age of seventy is in Huntsville, and so is the grave in which the hard-drinking old hero was buried. Sam Houston National Forest—one of four in East Texas—stretches for 250 square miles south and east of Huntsville.

Austin College—the second oldest in Texas, after Baylor—was established at Huntsville in 1849, on the campus of what is now Sam Houston State College. Later on it moved to Sherman, near the Oklahoma border above Dallas. But the original brick building that housed the older school, with its Jeffersonian Greek portico, is still in use. Known as Austin Hall, it is the social center for students at Sam Houston State. In a park on the grounds is the Sam Houston Memorial Museum, containing relics of the Republic's founder.

Huntsville also is the site of a notable institution of a different kind— the main unit of the State Penitentiary. It has a dozen units in all, the rest within 165 miles of Huntsville.

The State of Texas has always been rather lenient toward crime, except when it is manifested in its more lurid forms. The reason lies not

TV antennae atop cells
at Huntsville Penitentiary

Inmates compete in
Huntsville Prison Rodeo

so much in sentiment, or in the psychiatric theory that criminals are misunderstood, as in a simple recognition of the fact that violence is frequently a part of human life. Besides, Texans feel that being confined at all is punishment enough for most crimes.

The prison at Huntsville certainly isn't a place you might choose to spend a prolonged vacation. On the other hand, it is a reasonably healthy and enlightened place to be detained. Besides the automobile license-plate dispensary, it has the usual shops and other facilities to keep the prisoner's mind occupied and his hands busy. There is a chapel, a library, and a school. Among the sights that entertain visitors are the TV antennas on the roof above the cell blocks.

One unique feature of the Huntsville Penitentiary is the annual rodeo. The prison has its own baseball park. Every Sunday in October, the park is converted into a rodeo ring, and the prisoners put on exhibitions of riding, roping, and dogging steers. Since there is no principle in nature that prevents cowhands from running afoul of the law, the inmates normally include a number of accomplished performers. East Texas people come to the prison in droves to view one of the best rodeos in the state— and the penitentiary takes in about $100,000 in admissions, which are added to the prisoners' recreation funds.

82   This part of East Texas on the whole is a bucolic land, where people enjoy old-fashioned pleasures. Although new industries have sprung up here and there, as at Rockdale, they are concentrated mainly in the large port cities to the south, along the Gulf Coast. Most of the interior consists, as it did in the past, of plowed fields, meadows, and forest. Fishing is good in the lakes, streams, and bayous. Game birds are plentiful in the fall. Foxes roam the woods. A favorite community sport in East Texas is fox hunting—not on horseback, wearing red coats, Virginia style, but afoot with guns, in the manner of an African safari. There is even an organization to promote this pastime—the Texas Fox and Wolf Hunters' Association.

Another kind of community entertainment, indigenous to the countryside, is the old-time fiddlers' meeting. Like strolling minstrels in medieval Europe, these musicians go from town to town in spring and summer, competing for prizes and playing for youthful square dancers. Two of the best known fiddlers' meetings are at Crockett, northeast of Bryan, and at Athens, up toward Dallas.

Oldtime fiddlers' contest at Crockett

Bill Cooksey—Houston

Watermelons in a field in Robertson County

Like every other part of the state, East Texas has its favorite farm products. The area around La Grange, in Fayette County, leads the state in hogs, with more than 18,000. They fatten on the rich Fayette corn crop, which ranks fifth in Texas. The old settlements near Hempstead, Navasota, Wheelock, and Crockett are proud of their watermelons. Texans rarely get to see them, except while they are ripening in the fields. As with nearly all the major food crops of Texas, the best are packed and shipped to markets in the East. Only enough remain on small farms to supply the roadside stands that tempt motorists on the highways in August.

Travelers heading north through the Piney Woods, from Houston to the lumber capital at Lufkin, pass by the town of Moscow, which has about 200 inhabitants. They are philosophical about people who stop to ask them, "How's Khrushchev?"

Aside from the oddity of its name, Moscow is celebrated as the western terminal of the shortest operating railroad in Texas, if not in the

Mowan

Pulpwood trucks enter Southland Mills at Lufkin

nation. It is the Moscow, Camden & San Augustine, which connects Moscow with the somewhat larger town of Camden, a furlong less than seven miles away. If the line ever had any intention of going on to San Augustine (which is sixty miles northwest of Camden) it gave up the idea long ago. But it links Camden's 1,131 citizens to a branch of the Southern Pacific at Moscow.

The line was built back in the nineteenth century as a logging road for lumber interests in Camden. The logging operation moved on, and eventually became motorized; but the railroad was convenient for passengers and freight, and so it remained in service. Almost all the land over which it travels belongs to the lumber company, which also owns the sawmill, the only store, the hotel, restaurant, power plant, and most of the homes in Camden.

The schedule of the MC&SA consists of one trip daily in each direction, five days a week. The train is made up normally of several nondescript freight cars and a combination coach and baggage car with antique cane seats. The engine is an archaic Mogul, built in 1906 for service in the Panama Canal Zone. It was converted from steam to oil, and sold to the MC&SA in 1922.

At the Moscow terminus the cars are detached and the locomotive is turned by hand on an ancient turntable. Then the cars are hooked on again, the passengers come aboard, and the train winds its way back to Camden through the sunny fields and forest.

One of the things that attracted the pioneers to this region of Texas was its timber. Unlike the Spaniards, who lived in houses of stone and adobe, the Anglo-American settlers built their homes first of logs, and later of seasoned lumber. The first Texas sawmill was established at San

Augustine in 1825. It was operated—literally—by horsepower. Over the next eighty-five years, the lumber business grew into an industry turning out some two billion board feet a year.

As the timber resources were gradually exhausted, lumbering began to decline. A combination of forest depletion, drought, and building stagnation had reduced it to a mere 350 million board feet by the depression year 1932.

Since then it has revived. East Texas now cuts more than a billion board feet of lumber every year—about the amount that it produced at the start of the century, when the MC&SA was in its heyday. One important factor has been the adoption by the larger companies of modern conservation practices, under the guidance of forestry experts at Texas A&M.

An even more vigorous nudge was given to the reawakening East Texas lumber industry in the 1930's, when the late Georgia chemist, Dr.

Lake scene in a forest near Lufkin

Charles H. Herty, found a practical way to manufacture newsprint paper from yellow pine.

It takes half a century or more to renew the forests of Canadian spruce that once supplied most of the woodpulp for American newspapers. The Piney Woods of East Texas grow a new generation in twelve to sixteen years. They cover an area of about 30,000 square miles—roughly the size of Maine or South Carolina—in which two-thirds of the timber is yellow pine, and the rest hardwood such as oak or gum, which is more suitable for building, furniture, and most other purposes.

The Southland Paper Mills, at Lufkin, introduced the manufacture of newsprint to this part of the country. Opened in 1940, they have expanded several times, and now produce roughly 325,000 tons of newsprint each year.

The Champion Paper & Fibre Company, in Houston, specializes in fine paper stock for magazines and books, and also in kraft paper for brown grocery bags and wrapping.

A new plant at Evadale, near Beaumont, the East Texas Pulp & Paper Company, concentrates on the bleached white sulphite paper which is used for the printing of photographs in magazines.

Together, these three paper mills take about 60 per cent of the pulpwood harvested in East Texas. The balance goes to mills in Arkansas and Louisiana.

And the forest is growing. Scientific methods of cutting and replanting have increased its yield in the last twenty years or so, from 2,660 to nearly 3,000 board feet per acre. The return of prosperity to the lumber business has induced farmers to abandon food crops, and to stock their fields with trees instead. The Piney Woods around Lufkin have grown about 9 per cent in area, and East Texas is turning into a sylvan land again.

One part of it needs no restoration. It is the wild tangle of woods, underbrush, and jungle vines, covering about 3,000 square miles, known as the Big Thicket. Although it is in the middle of the lumber country, southeast of Moscow and Camden, it has resisted any inroads by the sawmill or the logging camp. A state highway between the towns of Woodville and Livingston skirts the northern edge of the Big Thicket. It passes through the only Indian reservation in Texas.

There never were a great many Texas Indians. They vanished before the white men, disappearing into Mexico or onto reservations in Oklahoma, leaving no trace except for a few lonely burial mounds like the ones at Alto, near Nacogdoches.

Highway Department

Indian burial mound near Alto

A single band of Alabama and Coushatta tribesmen—immigrants from the East—remained along the Neches River. They were given a small tract of land on the rim of the Big Thicket in 1854, at the suggestion of Sam Houston, who had been adopted by the Cherokee Indians in his youth. There they live today—some 300 of them—on a preserve that now totals about seven square miles.

On the whole, Texas has treated its minority citizens with more impartiality than is common in some of the states next to it. East Texas, where the great majority of Negroes live, has resisted integration of colored children into its public schools, but without the bitterness and violence that characterize race relations in the South.

The Negro school system is more than adequate, if not always quite up to the standards of white schools. Its 9,875 teachers and administrators earn salaries commensurate with those of white educators.

Texas has two state colleges for Negroes. Texas Southern University in Houston offers liberal-arts and professional courses; Prairie View A&M at Hempstead gives technical instruction. Texas at least is trying to meet its obligation to all its people. As well as a white observer can judge, Texas Negroes acknowledge and commend the effort.

Highway Department

Oil derricks in the heart of Kilgore

*T*HERE was a time—not so many years ago—when, if you were to draw an imaginary line between Waco and Nacogdoches, the part of East Texas above it looked very much like the part below it. Both were drowsy, comfortable, and largely rural. An elderly man named C. M. Joiner—known as "Dad"—changed all that. In October 1930, on the Daisy Bradford farm in Rusk County, about forty miles north of Nacogdoches, Dad Joiner struck oil.

It wasn't the first oil ever found in Texas. The great gusher at Spindletop, near Beaumont, back in 1901, had opened up the vast liquid store of subterranean wealth. But Dad Joiner's discovery turned out to be bigger than any pool of oil that had been tapped before. It extended under five counties around the cities of Tyler, Kilgore, and Longview. In the next twenty-seven years it yielded more than 3½ billion barrels of petroleum, and it is still producing, though not so prolifically as it once did.

Dad Joiner was seventy years old when he brought in the East Texas oil field. Born in Alabama, he had gravitated into Texas by way of Oklahoma, where he had already won and lost a couple of fortunes in oil. Geologists for the big companies had surveyed the area around Rusk County more than a dozen times before, and had reported definitely that it was dry. But Dad Joiner had his own mysterious method of deciding where oil was, and he had made up his mind that it was down there below the Daisy Bradford farm.

He had sunk two holes before this one, without finding anything. In order to drill the third, he had borrowed a rig, paying the company—and his workmen too—in pieces of the well. That wasn't hard to arrange, because the great depression had just settled on the land, and there were plenty of idle hands and equipment around. The well went down to 3,400 feet, and Dad was ready to give up for good when the black geyser burst high above the derrick, and cascaded over the bare fields beside it.

Daisy Bradford No. 3 blew in one year to the day after the stock market collapse of 1929. It saved Texas from the worst pangs of the depression, and started a boom that has lasted to this day. In effect, Texas has been immune to the economic tides advancing and receding over the rest of the nation. Its only serious worries are the world supply of petroleum, the need to regulate its own production, and the possibility that its reserves might run dry. They haven't yet.

Dad Joiner's Legacy

As for Dad Joiner, he moved to Dallas, where he spent his time fighting the 150 law suits that were brought against him after he struck it rich. Some of the suits were filed by his children, after he divorced their seventy-year-old mother, his first wife. At seventy-seven, Joiner was married again, to a young woman who had worked for him in the oil fields. When he died in Dallas ten years later, he was broke except for a few bits of almost worthless real estate.

If he had nothing else to bequeath, Dad Joiner left the face of this region changed beyond recognition. Oil and gas refineries followed the wells into Northeast Texas; pipe lines reached out toward the fuel-hungry cities on the Atlantic coast; drilling supply companies moved in; manufacturers built plants to produce machinery; and the area from Palestine to Jacksonville, from Tyler to Marshall, became an industrial section.

Not that there aren't plenty of rural corners left in it. This part of Texas also has its fields and forests, its wooded lakes where birds and fish abound. Caddo Lake, over on the Louisiana border—only thirty miles or so from the oil field—is the largest natural body of fresh water in Texas. It covers about sixty square miles in Caddo Lake State Park, bordered by cypress trees and swamp. Another big lake, formed by a dam across the Sulphur River, is up in the direction of Texarkana.

The Piney Woods reach into this part of Texas too, and are cut for timber. Farms are scattered over the landscape, producing much the same crops that are found to the south and west of Nacogdoches. But the look of the countryside is different. Most of it is urban. The towns and cities are closer together than they are elsewhere in Texas, and there are many more of them.

Long before Dad Joiner—in fact, even before Spindletop—Northeast Texas was reaching out toward its industrial destiny. The original Texas oil well was drilled as long ago as 1895 in Corsicana, southeast of Dallas, by a group of citizens who had been looking for water. It led to the construction—three years later—of the first oil refinery west of the Mississippi River, producing kerosene and a small amount of gasoline, for which there was practically no use at the time. The refinery eventually grew into the huge Magnolia Petroleum Company.

The old refinery was long ago dismantled. The site became a tank farm and pumping station for crude oil from other fields. But the historic still that cooked the oil is preserved in Corsicana, with a bronze tablet beside it to mark the birth of the Texas oil industry.

Still earlier, in the eighteen-seventies, East Texas had visions of becoming a great iron center, working the ore that runs through the same

region where oil was later found in such prodigious quantities. In Cherokee County—only a few miles from Dad Joiner's discovery well—the town of New Birmingham sprang up around the iron foundries.

It flourished for a time, along with the nearby town of Rusk, producing up to 50,000 tons of pig iron yearly. But lack of ready fuel finally drove New Birmingham's furnaces to import coke, and that made the iron too expensive. The industry gave up around 1900, and New Birmingham faded off the map. Not even a bronze tablet now identifies the spot where it stood.

Other iron works had similar experiences, without causing the death of whole communities. But one ancient blast furnace of Civil War days has survived as a monument, even though its economic life ended almost a century ago. It is the old Hughes Furnace that once was operated at Hughes Springs, near Daingerfield in the northeast corner of Texas. Restored a few years ago, it was removed to Lone Star, seven miles away, and placed beside a commemorative marker on the grounds of a successor industry, the Lone Star Steel Company.

The Lone Star plant is another striking example—and a more recent one—of the persistence of East Texas in its drive toward industrialization. It was organized in the early nineteen-forties, to supply the World War II defense plants burgeoning around the Gulf Coast, and cost $24,-000,000, most of it put up by the United States government. Before the steel mill could be completed, the war ended. The unfinished plant was offered for sale at $7,500,000 as a war-surplus property.

An elderly Dallas financier, John William Carpenter, who had long ago established the first electric power company in Texas, took it upon himself to make Lone Star Steel a going concern. For years he had been urging Texas to industrialize in a big way, and this was a golden opportunity to lay the solid foundation of an industrial economy.

In a ten-day series of public rallies around East Texas, Carpenter and his friends raised $1,500,000 in cash, to show the War Assets Administration that they had the means to operate Lone Star. They got the plant, and put it into production in 1947, turning out pig iron—like the vanished foundries of New Birmingham—in a 1,200-ton blast furnace.

The steel mill was completed in 1953, and has been enlarged since then. It converted the village of Lone Star overnight into a thriving industrial town. Lone Star Steel avoided the economic dilemma that had baffled its predecessors, half a century earlier, by building only fifty miles away from Oklahoma, which has the coal that Texas lacks. The mill gets its iron ore from mines in its own neighborhood, and brings in coal to stoke the furnaces.

94   Lone Star Steel has had its problems. What steel company doesn't? But it has also prospered. In the spring of 1960, when steel production over the country as a whole was being cut back, Lone Star paid a dividend of 10 per cent in stock. It would have paid in cash, but the government won't let it, so long as it owes the United States for loans which once totaled $87,000,000 and now come to about $32,000,000.

In April 1961, Lone Star decided to borrow the money privately, so that it can pay off the loan, declare regular dividends, and apply for a listing on the New York Stock Exchange. One of Lone Star's advantages over its giant competitors in the East is that it has no labor problem. While the big steel companies were closed down by the striking Steel Workers' Union in the last months of 1959, Lone Star went right on filling orders.

Its nonunion hands were fishing in Lone Star Lake—the big reservoir that supplies water to the plant—but not because they were idle. The company believes in a paternalistic policy of keeping its workers happy, and provides recreation facilities at the lake.

A good many of the newer industries in East Texas nowadays manufacture steel to fit their own needs. One is R. G. Le Tourneau, Inc., which

Old Hughes blast furnace at Lone Star

Steel worker fishing in Lone Star Lake

builds enormous earth-moving machines in a plant at Longview. Le Tourneau turns out more than 100,000 tons of steel a year in three electric furnaces, and fabricates them into parts for gigantic bulldozers that shove mountains aside, flatten forests, and push highways through the wilderness.

The largest piece of road-grading equipment ever constructed is a mammoth scraper, built by Le Tourneau, that gathers up 140 tons of earth in one load. The first of these dinosaurs arrived in Chantilly, Virginia, in the summer of 1959, to level runways for Washington's new Dulles International Airport. On it was a sign that read, "Made in Texas by Texans."

Robert G. Le Tourneau, who created this monster, is a Texan by adoption. Born in Vermont more than seventy years ago, of French Huguenot stock, he started out as a garage mechanic in California before World War I. A talent for inventing devices to improve road-building machinery got him into the business. By the end of World War II he had plants scattered over the United States, and a branch in Australia.

In 1953 Le Tourneau sold his earth-moving equipment firm to the Westinghouse Air Brake Company for $31,000,000. Then at the normal retirement age of sixty-four, he agreed not to build any more bulldozers for five years, by which time Westinghouse probably figured he would be content to putter around his home in Longview, watching television.

But Le Tourneau kept two of his plants, in Longview and in Vicksburg, Mississippi, making other kinds of heavy construction machinery while he waited out the five years of supposed rest. When they expired in 1958, he promptly brought out a new scraper with a capacity of seventy tons—which was two and half times the size of any then on the market—and followed it up a year later with the 140-ton behemoth.

Le Tourneau pioneered the use of electric motors to deliver power to the wheels. He now builds an individual motor into each wheel—deriving its energy from a central diesel—so that exactly the right amount of traction is exerted at each point where it is needed.

At the Vicksburg plant he builds a three-legged drilling platform for offshore oil. Self-propelled, the platforms float themselves into position, drop their legs, and hoist their decks above the surface in water as deep as 100 feet. They have been sold to oil companies as far away as the Persian Gulf.

Like many another Texas industrialist, Robert Le Tourneau has put the greater part of his fortune—including 90 per cent of his company stock and the dividends it pays—into a nonprofit foundation, to carry on educational and missionary activities. The foundation operates the Le

R. G. Le Tourneau leans on his equipment

Mammoth Le Tourneau road-grading machine

Le Tourneau plant at Longview

Tourneau Technical Institute in Longview, a junior college where the students supplement their academic studies by working in the Le Tourneau plant.

At the headwaters of the Amazon River in Peru, the foundation has a 1,500-square-mile plantation, on which it teaches the Indians modern farming and manufacturing methods. In Liberia, on the West Coast of Africa, it has a similar tract of nearly 1,000 square miles.

The company maintains a fleet of ten airplanes, manned by three pilots, to carry Le Tourneau on inspection tours of these and other projects. Because the landing field at the farm in Liberia has no kitchen, Le Tourneau has been known to get up before dawn and fly across the Atlantic to Brazil for breakfast.

Needless to say, the majority of East Texas enterprises are rather more prosaic than the widespread activities of Robert Le Tourneau. They consist of such normally productive facilities as the General Electric plant at Tyler, thirty-five miles west of Longview.

This GE branch makes air-conditioning equipment, which is considered as essential in Texas, during the long, hot summers, as furnaces are in the East, during the long, cold winters. GE is only one of more than 140 manufacturers in Tyler, the largest city between Dallas and Shreveport, Louisiana.

Though its economy is largely industrial, Tyler is better known as an agricultural center for one of the most fascinating farm crops produced in Texas: roses. From early spring until autumn, the flat fields around Tyler are redolent with the scent of roses, growing like cotton on vast, mechanized plantations.

Smith County harvests about twenty million rose bushes every year, shipping them to nurseries over the country. Eventually they wind up in suburban gardens, or as cut flowers boxed in green tissue paper with sprays of delicate fern.

The cultivation, packaging, and shipping of roses brings Tyler more than $7,000,000 a year, and the city makes the most of its unique product. The Municipal Rose Garden shows off massed banks of roses all summer. During the winter it nurtures them in greenhouses. In the spring they are replaced briefly by azaleas and camellias.

Private homes and public offices in Tyler are likely to be festooned with roses, as buildings in other places are decked with flags. In October, shortly before the first frost, Tyler puts on its annual Texas Rose Festival,

Rose crop in a field near Tyler

R. L. F

Queen of the Tyler Rose Festival

a three-day round of parades, exhibitions, ceremonies, and receptions approaching San Antonio's Fiesta San Jacinto in civic splendor. In Tyler, the roses on the Queen's float are real.

In addition to all that, citizens of Tyler can entertain themselves at either of two handsome parks. To the south is the new city-owned Lake Tyler Park, built around a reservoir covering four square miles, with facilities for swimming, boating, and games.

To the north—for those who prefer a more sylvan retreat—is Tyler State Park, a small but uncrowded resort in the woods. It has a tiny lake for fishermen, an outdoor dance pavilion, and camping sites. All around Tyler are streams and forests where hunters in autumn can find waterfowl, quail, and doves, deer and squirrels.

Much farther north, toward the Red River, the towns get smaller again, and the industrial development less noticeable. That part of East Texas, like the pioneer country below Nacogdoches, is largely rural, depending on agriculture, timber, and cattle. The Piney Woods give way to hardwood forests of oak and hickory, walnut, and especially bois d'arc— "wood of the bow" in French—that durable tree whose orange-colored grain was favored by early settlers for wagon axles.

The commercial center of this area is Paris, a neat, modern city with some plants making furniture, crates and boxes, and machinery. But the most influential community in the Red River Valley is Bonham, thirty-five miles west of Paris. Bonham has no industries of any great consequence, and only about 7,500 people. But one of the 7,500 is the Honorable Sam Rayburn, Speaker of the United States House of Representatives.

Speaker Rayburn has been a representative from his state longer than any other person in history. If he serves through one more full term in the House, until the spring of 1963, he will have been a member of that body for almost exactly half a century. (The anniversary will fall short of fifty years by two months, because the inauguration of a new Congress has been moved up to January since Rayburn was sworn in for the first time on March 4, 1913.) There is no reason why he shouldn't. Not only is the Speaker hale and vigorous on the verge of eighty; also he is one of the most warmly regarded congressmen who ever cast a vote or banged a gavel—by his associates as well as by his own constituents, who sent him there.

Rayburn grew up in the cotton fields outside of Bonham. He was one of eleven children of a farmer from Tennessee. A quick, bright boy, he decided early that he was going to be a lawyer and get himself elected to Congress. He attended what is now East Texas State College at Com-

Municipal Rose Garden, Tyler

merce, only twenty miles away from home, in the next county. After practicing law for a few years, he won his first election to Congress when he was thirty.

Rayburn never forgot what it was like to hoe cotton, or to ride over tooth-shaking roads to town in autumn on the tail gate of a wagon. His proudest achievement in Washington was to put through the rural electrification program in the 1930's, and next to that was the system of farm-to-market highways that crisscross Texas today.

Like George Perry, he became a convert to the idea that East Texas needed more cattle and less cotton—and led the way by founding the Sam Rayburn Model Hereford Ranch near Bonham. Mighty near everything around Bonham—including the public library—is named for the Speaker and has felt the warmth of his beneficent influence.

Needless to say, the rest of his Congressional District has not suffered. Made up of seven counties north and east of Dallas (including Rockwall, the smallest in Texas), it has within it two sizable cities, Sherman and Denison. They are only seven miles apart—and both are flanked by Air Force bases.

The birthplace of President Eisenhower, in a small frame house at Denison, has been restored and turned into a state park. It draws several thousand awed visitors each year. Mr. Eisenhower himself has gone back twice to refresh his childhood recollections.

Just north of Denison, where the Red River meets the Washita, is Sam Rayburn's most majestic monument, Lake Texoma. Covering 225 square miles between the rust-colored hills of Texas and Oklahoma, it supplies two of the most prized commodities in that generally dry land—power and lots of water.

6: Dallas the Cultured

y Howe, Jr.

Skyline of Dallas

IF San Antonio is the most intriguing city of Texas, Dallas without question is the most elegant. San Antonio has the homely charm of objects which are old and well-worn. Dallas is a bright, modern municipality that looks as if it might have come straight out of a showcase at Neiman-Marcus.

And this is as it should be, for Dallas is pre-eminently a merchandising city. Everything in it—including the tall buildings that rise up out of the prairie—could be said to exist for the primary purpose of displaying the opulence of Texas. San Antonio leans toward the ease and mellowness of life below the border. Dallas tends to be cosmopolitan and smart.

Though it ranks well behind Houston in size, with less than 700,000 people inside its corporate limits, against almost a million in Houston, Dallas is the business and financial capital of Texas. It is a city of banks, investment houses, and company headquarters, comparable to New York City, whereas Houston is an industrial center like Detroit.

That the Detroit of Texas should be larger than its Manhattan is not really so remarkable. The balance of enterprise in Texas still is on the side of production rather than management, of resources rather than marketing. But Dallas has been doing its concerted best in recent years to reverse the balance.

Even now, a truer picture of the relative sizes of the two cities is reflected in their metropolitan areas. There, Dallas has over a million residents, compared with about a million and a quarter in Houston. Conceivably, the day might come when Dallas—not Houston—will be the great metropolis of Texas.

How this inland city on the plains, without any major industrial resources of its own, made itself into a fiscal and commercial power is a story of some interest—though it lacks the drama of San Antonio's colorful past. It began, appropriately, with a trader from Tennessee, John Neely Bryan, who settled on the edge of the Trinity River in 1841, approximately where the Commerce Street viaduct now crosses that muddy stream.

Bryan had intended to open an Indian trading post, but he found that most of the Indians in the neighborhood had quietly departed. So he operated a ferry, sold powder, lead, and whisky to the farmers trickling in from the East, and set about promoting a town to increase his business.

104

106   The one-room log cabin that Bryan first occupied was moved over to the Dallas County Courthouse some years ago, and rebuilt under a canopy to preserve it from the weather. It is practically the only historical landmark left in Dallas. The citizens treat it with the sentimental tolerance of a merchant prince for the humble shack in which he was born. It serves as a delicate reminder of their present greatness.

As for the original occupant, he sold the ferry and his real-estate interests to a pioneer capitalist, Alexander Cockrell, and later exiled himself among the Creek Indians, under the mistaken impression that he was wanted for murder. He died in 1887. Mrs. Bryan, whom he had married after he moved to Texas, lived until 1919, and died in Dallas.

From the beginning, Dallas has been linked with East Texas by ties of common origin and business interest, even though it is physically closer to the West. Like the settlers over toward Louisiana, the pioneer families around Dallas grew corn and garden crops, and raised a few hogs and chickens. After the Civil War, they turned to cotton because it could be sold for cash. Dallas was a trading town, in the middle of a thriving cotton country, so it naturally became a cotton market.

Ed Miley

Founder Bryan's cabin on the Courthouse lawn

But it also takes cash to raise cotton—for seed and supplies, and for the food the farmer would grow if he weren't growing cotton. Since the small cotton planters of East Texas lived mainly on credit between harvests, the enterprising merchants of Dallas organized banks to finance them—and to get relief from the individual burden of carrying their debts.

Other things contributed to the growth of Dallas—for example, the fact that it was situated at a natural crossroads where people met, traveling through Texas from north to south or from east to west. This happy circumstance—abetted by the promotional genius of the tradesmen—brought the railroads into Dallas, and later on the airlines.

But the main attraction was the banks. When oil supplanted cotton as the most rewarding product of East Texas, the wildcatters went to Dallas to get money with which to pay for their drilling rigs and crews. When industry moved in, Dallas had the capital to finance it.

No less than twenty-four banks do business in Dallas. Some of them are prosperous suburban institutions, called into separate being by a Texas law which forbids branch banking. The Republic National Bank is the largest in the Southwest, and one of the largest anywhere in the country. Its total assets come to more than a billion dollars. The First National Bank isn't far behind. As the greatest money market in this part of the world, Dallas is the home of the Federal Reserve Bank which oversees financial operations in Arizona, New Mexico, Oklahoma, Texas, and western Louisiana.

The banks have been indirectly responsible for another vast supply of funds in Dallas. Back in 1908, the Legislature passed a law requiring all insurance companies that do business in Texas to invest 75 per cent of their receipts within the state itself. For a time, most of the national companies withdrew in a huff, and Texas-chartered companies took their place.

Because Dallas had money, they opened their central offices there. Thus Dallas became the headquarters of at least 216 Texas-owned insurance companies, and the regional home of several hundred national ones, when they returned. Their combined investments contribute mightily to the solvency of Texas.

The biggest name in Dallas finance, naturally, is that of Fred F. Florence, board chairman of the huge Republic National Bank. But the banker who has wielded the most influence over that city for the past quarter of a century is an eighty-year-old dynamo of energy and enthusiasm, Robert Lee Thornton, who was born the son of a tenant farmer in the cotton fields beyond Fort Worth.

Howe, Jr.

Memorial Auditorium, Dallas

Dallas Theatre Center

y Howe, Jr.

THE KALITA HUMPHREYS THEATER

Automobile show at the State Fair of Texas

Quincy Howe, Jr.

Ford plant affixes "Made in Texas" sticker

Lo

When Bob Thornton was nine, he saw the State Fair at Dallas for the first time, and conceived an undying affection for both the fair and the city. At sixteen he gave up school and found a job as a clerk in a store at Bristol, not far from Dallas. At twenty-four, he became a traveling candy salesman, spending much of his time in Dallas. Finally, at thirty, he settled down in Dallas for good, and opened a book store.

The State Legislature passed a law giving free textbooks to children, and drove the book store into bankruptcy. For a while Thornton tried the mortgage business. In 1916 he borrowed $6,000 and opened what is now the Mercantile National Bank, on the second floor of a run-down office building. Today the Mercantile ranks No. 3 in Dallas, after the Republic and the First National. It has its own thirty-story office building.

The success of the Mercantile Bank was due largely to Bob Thornton's apostolic faith in the economic future of Dallas. It started off making purchase loans for taxicabs and delivery trucks, to independent operators who found the older banks too conservative for this kind of business.

It has been following the same optimistic principles ever since. In time the other Dallas banks came around to Thornton's way of thinking, and all of them—the banks, the businessmen, the city—have prospered together.

Back in the 1930's, Thornton conceived the Dallas Citizens' Council. Originally it was a select group of fifty civic-spirited bankers and merchants, who had decided that it wouldn't hurt to give the economic future of Dallas a little friendly shove. Its first big promotion was the lavish 1936 Texas Centennial celebration, built around the State Fair. Though it lost money, the Centennial made Dallas known to the rest of the nation. Also, it brought Bob Thornton an honor which he cherishes above financial power. In 1945 he became president of the State Fair of Texas. It has been his public playground for the last fifteen years.

After the Centennial, the Citizens' Council went on to become the invisible government of Dallas, devoted primarily to business and industrial growth. In 1953, it offered Thornton an even larger field than the fair in which to exercise his rare creative talent. Through the Citizens' Charter Association—an offshoot of the Council, formed to give Dallas a more businesslike political management—he was persuaded to run for mayor.

He won handily, and now is serving his fourth term. Mayor Thornton is the symbolic figure who presides at municipal ceremonies and sells Dallas to the world at large from his office in the Mercantile Bank. The details of administration are handled efficiently, under the scrutiny of the Citizens' Council, by the city manager.

Dallas has always spoken with the most effective voice to keep the ownership, management, and finance of Texas industry at home. As a state whose economy is built mainly on its natural resources, Texas has found that its most formidable problem is to hold onto them, so that control of its wealth doesn't drift away to other places.

Back in the days of great cattle kingdoms, many of the greatest belonged to absentee proprietors in Scotland or England. Control of the big oil companies that grew like chains of molecules after Spindletop, spreading into regions as remote as Venezuela or the Persian Gulf, soon passed beyond the borders of Texas to the international financial centers of the world. Thus Texaco, which originated in Texas and was the ninth-ranking U.S. industrial corporation in 1958, now has its headquarters in New York City.

Some 2,500 publicly owned companies carrying on industrial operations in the United States are of such importance that the current prices of their stocks are regularly quoted by *The Wall Street Journal*. In spite of the vast growth of Texas industry over the past two or three decades, only sixty-five companies on this roster have their home offices in Texas.

Although Dallas ranks second to Houston in size and industrial development, twenty-five of these corporations are headquartered in Dallas, against twenty in Houston. The rest are scattered about the state.

Nearly all the Houston companies are in petroleum or related industries. But Dallas has a wide diversity of manufacturing, mining, and service activities. They include half a dozen oil companies, several major transportation systems, aircraft, electronics, food, steel, and utilities, as well as a host of miscellaneous businesses.

Eleven of the largest are listed on the New York Stock Exchange. In approximate order of size, they are Dresser Industries, Texas Instruments, Chance Vought Aircraft, Texas Utilities, Ling-Temco Electronics, Lone Star Gas, Braniff Airways, Texas & Pacific Railway, General American Oil, TXL Oil, and Dr. Pepper, a soft drink.

The rise of Dallas in banking and commerce naturally made it a transportation center. The Texas & Pacific, reaching from Louisiana to El Paso, with extensions over North Texas, follows one of the historic highways across the state from east to west. (The other, through San Antonio, is the route of the Southern Pacific, which has its home office in San Francisco.)

Braniff Airways moved to Dallas almost thirty years ago from Oklahoma, where it started as a local line between Oklahoma City and Tulsa. Today it runs as far east as New York City, north to Minneapolis and St. Paul, west into Denver, and south all the way to Buenos Aires. It ranks among the largest airlines in the nation.

The emphasis on finance and trade in Dallas is reflected in some of the businesses which have settled there. In many cases, they are firms relying less on vast production than on finesse in organization and management. The aircraft and electronic firms—and Dresser Industries—are typical in this respect. In one way or another they belong to the new industrial era that has developed since World War II.

Back in the old days, Dallas was a moderately important producer of cotton-gin machinery, and later had some textile mills and other random plants. But manufacturing wasn't really its specialty, and wouldn't amount to much today if the aviation industry in the Second World War hadn't picked Dallas and its environs as an ideal place to build aircraft.

One reason for the growth of airplane production was the proximity of so many large Air Force and Navy air bases. Another was the fine expanse of prairie in the neighborhood of Dallas and Fort Worth. Still another was the generally fair weather. Chance Vought and Temco were only two of the largest aircraft companies that settled around Dallas.

Both moved into Grand Prairie, an industrial extension of Dallas halfway toward Fort Worth. (Grand Prairie is almost indistinguishable from Arlington, which is an extension of Fort Worth halfway toward Dallas.) Chance Vought manufactures fighter aircraft and missiles for the Navy, and does some work on research rockets for the National Aeronautics and Space Administration.

Ling-Temco, formed in 1960 by a merger of Temco with James J. Ling's fast-rising electronic business in Dallas, makes a variety of airplanes, missiles, and components. But its main interest for several years has been in creating electronic guidance and communication systems for missiles and rocket vehicles.

In the spring of 1961, after a strenuous public courtship, Ling-Temco and Chance Vought announced their impending marriage. The merger would make them together one of the biggest companies in the aircraft-missile-electronics field. And it would put the benediction of success on the abrupt accession to financial leadership of thirty-eight-year-old James Ling.

In the most glamorous of postwar industries, Texas Instruments has been one of the most remarkable newcomers. Starting out in a modest way as a manufacturer of oil-exploration instruments, it has developed

114   into one of the top electronic laboratories of the space age. In the process, it has given a truly spectacular performance on the Stock Exchange.

Quoted at about $20 a share just a few years ago, Texas Instruments climbed steadily all through 1959 and the spring of 1960, when most other stocks were falling, until it sold for as much as $250. Quite a few Texans got richer than ever from a small flyer in Texas Instruments.

A different brand of business altogether is Dresser Industries. It is one of those fascinating rag quilts of modern corporate endeavor—a group of separate though related companies, put together under unified management and financial control. It began as a family enterprise in Pennsylvania, eighty years ago, making equipment for oil drillers and couplings for pipe lines.

At the height of the boom in the 1920's, the Dresser family sold it through a public issue of stock. A management expert, Neil Mallon—now chairman of the board—was brought in to run it. By a series of mergers with other corporations engaged in roughly similar activities, Mallon built Dresser Industries into the diversified operation it is today.

Under the present organization in Dallas are fifteen different companies doing business in California, Indiana, New York State, Ohio, Oklahoma, Pennsylvania, and Texas. In addition, there are twenty-two affiliated Dresser companies abroad. Their products range from drilling supplies to pumps, from seismographs for oil exploration to radar and TV antennas, from rocket-launching platforms to rare kinds of mud, used in digging holes in the ground.

Dresser Industries moved to Dallas because a large part of its domestic market—and seven of its operating units—are in Texas. It adds quite an air of financial importance to that city, whose largest industries at one time were the Ford assembly plant (where cars and trucks are "Built in Texas by Texans") and the shops of Braniff Airways.

The part of Dallas that most visitors see first is the airport. Dallas does its level best to make that first impression a favorable one. The new air terminal at Love Field cost $45,000,000, and provides a separate air-conditioned waiting room for each flight. Dallas had the first jet service in Texas, by American Airlines to New York, its most traveled route. Airline operators in Dallas are more attentive than in most cities to the passenger's comfort and safety.

An easterner who passed through Dallas not long ago tells a story that helps to explain how Dallas got where it is today. He had boarded a rather tired but apparently serviceable DC-7 in Florida, bound for Los Angeles. On the way into New Orleans, one of the engines had quit. A

Shelton

Manager James F. Albright in Cokesbury's vast book store

mechanic wandered out to meet the plane with a screw driver in his hand, and tinkered with the engine for a while. Then the passengers got aboard again, all four engines started up, and they went on to Dallas.

At Love Field, while the easterner was in the washroom, the airplane disappeared. He went back to find the passengers waiting, while a wiry, weathered Texan in coveralls explained, "We've taken that old airplane away, folks. Somebody kicked a hole in the side of it. We're sending for another one to fly you on to L.A."

The easterner had a mental image of the Dallas crew wheeling the old airplane away and dropping it over the side of a ravine in disgust, while they ordered a fresh one from Neiman-Marcus. The Texan kept shaking his head and asking with a wry smile, "Now, who would want to do a thing like that—kick a hole in the side of an airplane?"

Presently the replacement rolled up to the gate—a silvery Flagship, looking as if it had just been removed from a Christmas gift wrapping. While it was being gassed and inspected with pride by the Dallas crew, the hostesses loaded the galley with champagne and caviar canapes. A few minutes later the passengers climbed aboard and took off for Los Angeles—an hour late, but in high spirits, riding Texas style.

Nobody who knows Dallas will doubt that the story is true. Dallas is the city where a women's clothing store on the trackless prairie made itself into one of the smartest fashion centers in America. Neiman-Marcus, more than any other single institution, typifies the way things are done in Dallas. Sheer imagination, guided by the merchandising genius of the late Herbert Marcus and his urbane son, Stanley Marcus, made Neiman-Marcus the best-known specialty store in America.

The success of Neiman-Marcus is founded on the firm conviction of Texans in general, and Dallas Texans in particular, that they don't need to go beyond the borders of Texas for anything—not even to Paris or New York for *la haute couture*. The brilliance of the Marcus family (there haven't been any Neimans in Neiman-Marcus for more than thirty years) lies in the fact that they understand this trait in Texans, and cater to it by bringing everything fashionable to Dallas, where they display it with superb showmanship.

As long ago as 1930, Neiman-Marcus became the first store of its kind to advertise in national magazines like *Vogue* and *Harper's Bazaar*. The idea was to impress Texans—but the result has been to convince a great many other people over the nation that a Neiman-Marcus label is the assay mark of style. Neiman-Marcus long since outgrew Dallas as a market. Its customers are everywhere. In its own field, it is a sort of national operation—a ladies' Dresser Industries.

Just before Christmas, 1959, a TV news analyst in Washington, Bryson Rash, went on the air one evening with a copy of the annual Neiman-Marcus gift catalogue in his hand. With the awe of a man exhibiting a rare first edition, he riffled through the pages, showing his audience a few of the things that Neiman-Marcus had for sale.

They included a prize Black Angus steer, delivered to the recipient's door on Christmas morning, along with a roasting cart, for $1,925. On the next page was an emerald-and-diamond necklace costing $100,000 (tax included) with matching earrings at only $30,000 more. An Empress chinchilla coat was offered for $25,000—as an accessory with a surrey-style jeep at $1,848.

Interspersed with these items were other trinkets—equally smart—that sold for $2.50 or $4.95. The Neiman-Marcus technique is to flaunt the luxury of its wares with engaging effrontery—but never to ignore a customer who wants something in good taste at a modest price. Neiman-Marcus exploits munificence, because Texans are charmed by princely gestures. But what it really sells is exquisite simplicity—the essence of style—which has no price.

This, in a way, is what all the public agencies in Dallas are up to, taking their cue from Neiman-Marcus. From the mayor's office to the newspapers, from the symphony to the book shops to the State Fair, they are all busy selling Dallas as a center of style in municipal government, in industry, in art, in culture, in entertainment. All of these things to-

gether add up to the sense that a city may have of its own quality. And **117**
Dallas thinks of itself as a living monument—a great city, worthy to be
named with Alexandria, Athens, Rome, and Florence among the timeless
habitations of history.

That is why it sells books with the same enthusiasm that it lavishes
on furs or necklaces, transistors, or drilling tools. The biggest book store
in the nation, if not in the world, is Cokesbury's in Dallas, a six-story
block of Georgia marble between Main and Commerce Streets, with
66,000 square feet of floor space. Under the astute management of James
F. Albright—who is a sort of impresario of books, as Stanley Marcus is
an impresario of decorative objects for ladies—Cokesbury sells more than
three million dollars' worth of books every year, and not only in Dallas.
Its mail-order market covers the entire Southwest.

Every now and then, Dallas puts on a book celebration that does for
current literature what the State Fair does for industry and commerce in
Texas. The last one was part of a five-week Festival of the Arts just before
Thanksgiving 1959. Texas authors were wined and dined, along with
such visiting soothsayers as Moss Hart, Kay Thompson, and the Duke of
Bedford. In charge, as usual, was the elegant dean of Dallas critics, Lon
Tinkle, escorted by the book editors of the Dallas newspapers—which
treat the written word almost as if it flowed richly out of the ground.

The Dallas "Morning News"

Quincy Howe, Jr.

The Dallas *Morning News* is one of two Texas papers that claim to speak for the state as a whole—meaning not only its total area, but its entire range of experience, as one speaks of a whole man. The other is the Houston *Post*. They feud with one another across the intervening 225 miles of prairie—especially over such vital questions as the advancement of music or painting in their respective provinces—while each endures the competition in its own neighborhood with comparative good humor. The competition in Dallas is the afternoon *Times Herald,* which looks upon the municipality around it with only a trifle less—if any—than the reverence shown by the *News.*

The Dallas *News* has a good reason to consider itself something more than just a local voice. It is one of the very few newspapers which have been transplanted, full-grown, from a distant spot to the one it now occupies. The *News* started in Galveston in 1842, only a year after John Neely Bryan put up the log hut that was to become Dallas. In 1885, its owners concluded that Dallas had matured enough to merit a metropolitan press. So they opened a branch office on the Trinity and brought out a Dallas edition.

For a while, the two papers were practically identical, exchanging stories by telegraph. But the Dallas edition outgrew its parent. In 1923, the Galveston *News* was sold, and they parted company.

In Texas nowadays the importance of a city is judged less by its wealth than by the size and prominence of its symphony orchestra. The Dallas Symphony can trace its origin back to 1900, when it was an amateur group trying to bring musical sophistication to the cotton capital of Texas. Reorganized after World War II, with lavish financial support by the culture-conscious citizens of Dallas, it is now among the dozen or so top orchestras in the nation.

Its musical director for several years was the Polish *émigré* conductor and composer, Paul Kletzki. When Dr. Kletzki returned to his home in Switzerland early in 1961, the Dallas Symphony lured Georg Solti away from the Los Angeles Philharmonic. His opening season in Dallas was to be 1961–62.

The Dallas Symphony—through a competition established in 1931 by the late publisher George B. Dealey of the Dallas *News*—claims the discovery in 1952 of Van Cliburn, the willowy young concert pianist from Kilgore, who went on to astonish everybody by winning the Tchaikovsky Prize in Moscow. The triumph of the orchestra's 1958–59 season was the return of Cliburn for a concert which was sold out long before the season began. Cliburn received the full civic social treatment, including a reception and dinner—with Speaker Sam Rayburn—at the Cipango Club.

Leo B. Johnson

Pianist Van Cliburn with Speaker Sam Rayburn at the Cipango Club

The Republic National Bank of Dallas

No public institution in Dallas typifies the city more sharply than the private Cipango Club, a sumptuous Mediterranean villa on a hill overlooking Turtle Creek, in the Cedar Springs area just north of the business district. It was founded in 1946 as an exclusive gambling resort for prodigal Texas oil men and industrialists. But lavish luncheon and dinner parties turned out to be more attractive to the clients than throwing their money away for nothing.

So the Cipango Club abandoned its games, and concentrated on expensive entertainment. Edward E. Zimmerman, one-time manager of the Brook Hollow Country Club, was brought in to run the Cipango. A former assistant attorney general of the United States, "Judge" John A. Erhard, was appointed chairman of the board. The Cipango Club today is not only as rich as the Citizens' Council, but equally respectable.

A good many of the elect in Dallas belong to both. Among them are, for example, Neil Mallon of Dresser Industries—which holds its annual Christmas party at the Cipango Club—and Stanley Marcus. Leo F. Corrigan Sr., who built a large part of present-day Dallas and owns a world-wide string of hotels stretching all the way to Hong Kong, is another. The family of the same Clint Murchison who helped his friend to buy the New York Central is represented in both groups. The younger Murchisons often entertain at the Cipango Club for such intimates from Hollywood as actor John Wayne and his wife Pilar.

The club has more than 1,000 members, of whom the poorest are certified by Dun & Bradstreet to be worth at least $100,000. In fact, Eddie Zimmerman has been quoted as saying that the club has little to offer anybody of less means. A goodly number of its patrons are nonresident— but highly solvent—people with names like Henry Ford II or Winthrop Rockefeller, who have business interests in Dallas.

The same sense of style that distinguishes Dallas in other respects is found in its educational services. Two honor graduates of Highland Park High School—Midshipman Alton K. Thompson and Cadet Charles Paddock Otstott—ranked at the top of the Class of 1960 at Annapolis and West Point, respectively. The most fashionable private school in Texas for young women is Hockaday in Dallas.

Young ladies at the Hockaday School

122 Southern Methodist University, despite its church affiliation, approximates the traditional concept of a liberal arts college more closely than any other institution of learning in the state. With its classic campus and its moderate enrollment of fewer than 6,000 students, Southern Methodist is able to provide a leisurely and thoughtful background for the intellectual experience of living.

Even in football, Southern Methodist is marked by style and brilliance rather than brute power. Its greatest players in recent years have been passing stars like Doak Walker and Don Meredith, who gave the team a kind of rapier-sharp alertness on the attack that was full of scintillating surprise and suspense. Southwest Conference football on the whole has lost this quality, in order to match the power of the teams which it meets in national competition. But at SMU the game still gives the impression of being played for sheer excitement.

Southern Methodist's home field is the Cotton Bowl, in Fair Park, an exhibition city on the eastern edge of Dallas. The park was created for the Texas Centennial Exposition, back in 1936. Since then it has been the home of the annual State Fair of Texas in October. Between

Midway at the State Fair of Texas

Squire Haskins

Squire Haskins

Texas Hall of State in Fair Park

124 fairs it serves handsomely as a cultural and economic center. Built around a spacious Esplanade with a reflecting pool down the middle, Fair Park is the Acropolis and the Forum of Dallas.

Its focal point is the monumental Hall of State, a $1,200,000 edifice of white marble in the shape of a T (for Texas). The Hall of State is a historical museum. Half a dozen enormous buildings at Fair Park provide nearly eight acres of floor space for industrial, agricultural, and technical exhibits. They are in frequent use for meetings.

The park has an auditorium seating 4,000 people; a theater; the Dallas Museum of Fine Arts; the Museum of Natural History; a health museum; an aquarium; a garden center; an outdoor amphitheater; an ice arena; a roller-skating rink; barns and livestock buildings; a picnic pavilion; a swimming pool; and several restaurants. One of the oddities of Fair Park is a monorail line, which carries passengers—in a car suspended from an overhead track—the quarter-mile from the gate to the entrance of the Cotton Bowl.

For sixteen days in the fall, while the State Fair is in progress, these exhibition halls and places for amusement swarm with more than

Exhibiting a pony at the State Fair

Quincy Howe, Jr.

THE LONE STAR OF TEXAS HAS PASSED ON AND BECOME FIXED IN THAT GLORIOUS CONSTELLATION WHICH ALL FREEMEN AND LOVERS OF FREEDOM MUST REVERENCE AND ADORE · THE AMERICAN UNION

Giant gold medallion in the Texas Hall of State

2,500,000 Texans. The State Fair of Texas has been known as the largest in the nation ever since 1888, two years after it was founded. By now it has grown so big that it no longer deserves to be ranked as a state festival at all. It is more like a permanent world's fair, honoring the greatness of Dallas.

There is seemingly no limit to the hunger of Dallas for metropolitan growth and recognition. For twelve decades the citizens of this inland community have been united in a single-minded endeavor, to make Dallas the foremost city of the Western world. Theirs is something much more impressive than the simple itch for expansion that is found in most of the young municipalities of America. For reasons which are hidden from the scrutiny of a casual eye, Dallas wants to be—and in its own mind is—the market place of twentieth-century civilization.

While other cities concentrate on some one specialty, such as oil or

126   cattle, steel or automobiles, finance or fashions, retail business or entertainment, Dallas concentrates merely on greatness. It includes every kind of human activity in its province, and trades in all of them with equal enthusiasm.

That is why, though Houston has until now the biggest population, most people think of Dallas as the No. 1 city of Texas. Give it time, with plenty of leaders like Bob Thornton, and very likely it will be. There's lots of room on the plains.

7: Fort Worth, Where—

. Stryker

Cattle on a ranch near Fort Worth

*T*HE city limits of Dallas and Fort Worth are only about eight miles apart. The brief stretch of turnpike between them is largely occupied by the suburban towns of Grand Prairie and Arlington. It would be logical to expect that they would some day grow together into a single entity. Considered as one metropolitan complex, along with their neighboring satellites, right now they form an urban area of about 1,650,000 inhabitants, ranking among the ten most populous centers in the United States. Yet in spite of the fact that they are joined so intimately by their physical boundaries, no two cities could be more remote from one another in spirit.

Dallas belongs to the flourishing industrial community of East Texas. Fort Worth, as its motto proclaims, is where the West begins. Dallas originated as a cotton market and financial center for the farming area around it. Fort Worth started as a trading post for cattle drovers heading north along the Chisholm Trail.

That legendary highway ran almost due north toward Indian Territory from San Antonio, where the lean and hardy Longhorns assembled. It ended in Kansas, at the railheads in Abilene and later Wichita, where the travel-weary beasts were loaded on stock cars for shipment to hungry diners in the East. The route was laid out so that it would skirt the settled regions, where farmers had begun to fence the land. So it passed thirty miles west of Dallas, pausing briefly at the muddy crossing of the Trinity, where Fort Worth now stands.

For several years before the Civil War the site had been occupied by a small frontier Army station, known as Camp Worth. (It was later promoted by the inhabitants to the dignity of a fort.) The Indians had melted away, and the Army had long since departed, when the Chisholm Trail went through.

A handful of traders, who were left behind, had moved into the cluster of deserted buildings, converting the barracks into stores, the officers' quarters into houses, and the stables into a hotel. By a bit of high-handed political skullduggery, they got the trading post designated as the county seat.

Fort Worth was the last place of any consequence where supplies could be laid in, before the Red River crossing into the Indian Nation, seventy-five miles north. The town subsisted on cattle drives until 1876. Then it got a railhead of its own—though not without some effort.

Maze at the meeting of Interstate Highways 20 and 35

The Texas & Pacific, pushing west from Dallas, ran out of money in the neighborhood of what is now Grand Prairie. The citizens of Fort Worth turned out in a body to lay the tracks, and extended the city limits a quarter of a mile to meet them. The first train chuffed into town just in time to avoid losing its land grant from the state.

With the railroad—and with a spider's web of other rail lines and highways that gradually converged on it—Fort Worth became a cattle market in its own right. Around the turn of the century, the stockyards were built. Meat-packing plants—the first in Texas—moved in with them, to convert the animals into beef and its by-products.

Today the livestock rolling into Fort Worth by rail and truck from all over North Texas are worth about $175,000,000 a year. Around $20,000,000 of that amount goes to Fort Worth's own people, for handling and processing the animals. They provide the city with the bawling strength of its economy.

Beef by itself isn't enough to account for the growth of Fort Worth into the fourth city of Texas—after Houston, Dallas, and San Antonio—with somewhat over 350,000 citizens inside its corporate limits. Beef alone doesn't explain, for example, the maze of modern highways into Fort Worth, culminating in the futuristic four-level cloverleaf where Interstate Highway 20—crossing the continent—meets Interstate Highway 35, which follows the old Chisholm Trail.

But beef has always been the basic source of revenue in Fort Worth, and has given the city its characteristic fiber and flavor. For that reason Fort Worth has been looked on with affection in the state as the most typical of Texas cities. Oil and industry are relatively new in Texas, and are still associated with the sections where they have appeared in the most obvious concentrations. But cattle are found everywhere within the borders of the state, and in increasing numbers over the past few years, as farmers have turned more and more from cotton or wheat to calves.

Fort Worth is the cattleman's metropolis. The feet that tread its paved streets are fitted into high-heel boots, which are better suited for dirt or dust; and the hats which are doffed in its sedate elevators downtown are Stetsons, better designed for keeping the sun off a man's face.

For many years Fort Worth has been the city home of ranchers, who built palatial mansions from the profits on their cattle preserves out in the wide open spaces. One of its showplaces is the town house of the late W. T. Waggoner, who ran 60,000 head of beef on half a million acres near Vernon, 150 miles northwest of Fort Worth, along the upper reaches of the Red River. Waggoner's Three-D Ranch was almost as rich in oil

132   as in cattle—and this mingling of cloven hooves with the aromatic essence of carbon also is characteristic of Fort Worth.

Another notable dwelling was the home of Burk Burnett, who bequeathed his name to the town of Burkburnett, above Wichita Falls, and to the oil field around it. Perhaps the most impressive of these town houses was the residence of Winfield Scott—no kin, so far as anybody can recall, to the Mexican War general, who was a Virginian. Scott was practically an early settler of Fort Worth. His ranch home was at Cresson, only twenty miles away. Along with the Waggoners and the Burnetts, he helped to make Fort Worth a city whose social life is dominated by the old-time cattle families of Texas.

Fort Worth is the headquarters of the Texas and Southwestern Cattle Raisers' Association. The most powerful organization of its kind anywhere, it includes some 10,000 breeders of blooded cattle in Texas, Oklahoma, and New Mexico.

Fort Worth's equivalent of the State Fair in Dallas is the nine-day Southwestern Exposition and Fat Stock Show at the end of January every year. It is held in the huge Will Rogers Memorial Coliseum that Fort Worth built in 1936 for its Frontier Exposition, as a rival attraction to the Centennial in Dallas.

The indoor rodeo which is the climax of the exposition is reputed to be the biggest in the country—bigger even than the one at Madison Square

Will Rogers Memorial Auditorium and Tower

Quincy Howe, Jr.

Home of the late cattleman Winfield Scott

Garden in New York. It is also the most important social affair of the year in Fort Worth, outranking the Civic Opera which takes the place of a major symphony orchestra. Both draw furtive patrons from Dallas, trying hard to look as if they came from some other place.

The Coliseum, with its companion tower and auditorium, is a monument to the friendship between the rope-twirling cow-country sage and humorist, Will Rogers, who died in an airplane crash in Alaska the year before it was dedicated, and the late Amon G. Carter Sr., publisher of the Fort Worth *Star-Telegram*. Amon Carter filled much the same role in Fort Worth that Mayor Bob Thornton has filled in Dallas. He was its No. 1 promoter, civic leader, and host. His trade-mark was the supply of ten-gallon Stetson hats which he passed out to visiting celebrities.

134   It was chiefly Amon Carter who kept alive the feud between Fort Worth and Dallas. He used to say that, on the rare occasions when business of an unavoidable nature drove him to visit the other city on the Trinity, he took his lunch along so that he wouldn't have to buy anything in Dallas.

Carter has been accused sometimes of carrying the rivalry with Dallas to extremes. But if he hadn't dramatized Fort Worth's impassioned individuality, the city might have been reduced long since to little more than an outlying suburb of Dallas. Instead, Fort Worth has identified itself as a flourishing industrial city in its own right.

Its expansion into the byways of industry hasn't been as noticeable as that of Houston or Dallas. The reason is simple. Fort Worth doesn't sit on top of some great natural resource like the oil and chemicals under Houston, nor has it stored away enormous sums of money in its banks, like Dallas. Its productive enterprises have grown up without any apparent pattern, and for no apparent purpose, except that the city was there, with its complex of railroads and highways.

An example of the seemingly random nature of Fort Worth's growth is provided by the Texas & Pacific itself—the railway that Fort Worth saved from becoming a branch line into Dallas, and which in turn made Fort Worth a cattle center. The main yards of the T&P are in Fort Worth today.

Shortly before World War II the company built a spacious twelve-

Christian Church at Texas Christian University

Quincy Howe, J.

Campus of Texas Christian University

136   story office building and terminal in Fort Worth. It was quickly occupied by other businesses, but the T&P never got around to moving in. Its headquarters remain in Dallas, where the money is.

On the other hand, Fort Worth is the home of the Champlin Oil & Refining Company, which started out as an investment business—the Chicago Corporation—and ended up operating its own oil fields and refineries, with $74,000,000 in sales in 1960. The big Ranger oil field, in nearby Eastland County, made Fort Worth a refining center as long ago as 1917. It still draws a good deal of the petroleum from wells farther west.

Fort Worth is a major processing point for grain. Flour mills and elevators loom above the plain north of the city. Some of its miscellaneous products are cottonseed oil, candy, trailers, farm equipment, fertilizers, and building materials. General Motors has an assembly plant in suburban Arlington, matching the Ford assembly plant at Grand Prairie.

The biggest single manufacturing activity in Fort Worth today is aircraft. Amon Carter is credited with having brought the vast Convair plant of General Dynamics to Fort Worth at the start of World War II. Occupying almost a square mile of prairie, with an assembly line four-fifths of a mile long, Convair's Fort Worth Division is said to be the largest aircraft factory in the world.

Fort Worth Public Health Center

Quincy H

Theater-in-the-round under dome of the Casa Mañana

For some years after the war, it was busy turning out mammoth six-engine B-36 bombers for the Air Force. Now that they are obsolete, it builds the jet B-58, which is considerably smaller but capable of supersonic speed. The B-58 is the most advanced airplane for offensive operations in the present arsenal of the Strategic Air Command.

Convair is nothing if not convenient to its customers. Right across the road is Carswell Air Force Base, one of the vital SAC bases from which the B-58 operates. From Carswell, long after Fort Worth is asleep, flights of jet bombers take off on world-wide practice missions, pinpointing targets (over friendly territory) that resemble the ones they might have to destroy in time of war.

The Convair plant has drawn a number of other aircraft manufacturers and producers of aircraft components to Fort Worth. The Bell

138   Aircraft Corporation builds helicopters at its Fort Worth branch. The Menasco Manufacturing Company makes landing-gear assemblies for airplanes. These and other units of the aviation industry around Fort Worth and Dallas make the whole area a significant one in national defense.

Almost exactly midway between Fort Worth and Dallas is a $12,000,000 monument to Amon Carter, and to his faith in the future of air travel—particularly air travel connecting Fort Worth and places more distant than Dallas. It is the Greater Fort Worth International Airport, better known as Amon Carter Field.

Originally it was conceived as a joint air terminal for Dallas and Fort Worth. Jealousy on both sides led Dallas to pull out and rebuild its own Love Field, about ten miles—or two minutes' flying time—closer to Dallas.

Amon Carter Field is one of the most handsome—and among the most tranquil—airports in America. The spacious Concourse looks more like the subdued lobby of a modern bank than like the busy heart of a transportation system. It is decorated with murals in bas-relief, showing episodes in the history of Texas. Inscriptions in gold leaf on these panels —by an unnamed author—remind the traveler that "deeds of the past and present are but stepping stones of the future," and that "the centuries pass—history alone, enduring, remains with us."

The terminal facilities at Amon Carter Field are as advanced as any in the country. There is plenty of room for jet runways on its three square miles of level land. Yet transcontinental flights generally pass it by these days, for the obvious reason that the fast new jets cannot afford to land at two airports practically side by side, and more passengers have business in Dallas.

In view of this fact, you might say with a good deal of justice that Amon Carter Field—be it ever so attractive—is a flagrant example of civic extravagance. On the other hand, you might say with equal justice that Fort Worth and Dallas both are fortunate in possessing two great airports, capable of serving their needs in air travel for some years to come.

Fort Worth's devotion to aviation, incidentally, has brought it one of the most glamorous educational institutions in Texas, or anywhere else. It is the unique Stewardess College of American Airlines, on a twenty-acre tract of wooded land next to the airport.

Although American Airlines is a national system with headquarters in New York City, it has a natural affinity for Texas, and Texans recipro-

Howe, Jr.

Botanic Gardens in Trinity Park

cate its feeling. The company spent a million dollars on the luxurious building of gray Texas fieldstone, where it trains personable young women in the gentle art of looking after nervous passengers.

It takes a corps of nearly 1,600 stewardesses to staff the fleet of American flagships, and the number keeps growing year by year, as the airplanes get bigger and more people use them. Jet airliners, which have now taken over nearly all the long-distance routes in the United States and abroad, carry as many as four stewardesses—three in the first-class section up forward, and one aft.

A representative member of this elite group stays with the company only twenty-seven months. Then she gets married and has to be replaced. American finds that it pays to give the replacement a thorough grounding in flight procedures, instead of wasting any of this precious time in training them on the job.

The airline interviews about 50,000 girls a year in Mexico, Canada, and the United States, to find the 800 or so whom it sends to Fort Worth for study, at its own expense. Chosen for their personality, health, intelligence, and enthusiasm—especially for flying—they receive a six-week course of instruction in subjects as various as meteorology, navigation, the theory of flight, serving meals, first aid in a medical emergency, personal grooming, and how to make pleasant conversation.

Twice during the term they fly as observers on scheduled runs, sometimes helping the regular stewardesses for practice. On their graduation, they get a chic blue uniform decorated with wings, and a job that pays handsomely, carries them about the world, and leads 85 per cent of them to the altar in no time at all.

Fort Worth has its full quota of more orthodox teaching centers. Texas Christian University is one of the half-dozen major founts of wisdom in the state. It is operated by the Disciples of Christ, a particularly strong denomination in this part of Texas, and is considered rather more strict in its behavior than other large church-supported schools.

Arlington State College belongs to Texas A&M. It has excellent resources for instruction, especially in engineering and business administration. Fort Worth is also the home of Texas Wesleyan College, the Southwestern Baptist Theological Seminary, and Our Lady of Victory, a select Catholic college for women.

Fort Worth is well provided with handy spots for boating and fishing, as most large Texas cities are today. Lake Worth and Eagle Mountain Lake both are formed by dams across the Trinity, contributing to Fort Worth's generous water supply.

Fort Worth, Where——

Lake Benbrook, on another fork of the Trinity, also belongs to Fort Worth. Grapevine Lake furnishes water to Dallas, but it is almost within hailing distance of Fort Worth. Lake Whitney, one of the largest in Texas, is just forty miles away.

The proximity of all these lakes has brought still another industry to Fort Worth—and an odd one it is for a landlocked city. Within an hour's drive are sixteen plants manufacturing boats. They turn out more than 40,000 small craft a year, for which boating enthusiasts around Fort Worth pay $25,000,000.

141

Burrus Flour Mills and grain elevator

Smith

142   Within the city are places for recreation of a less expensive kind. Fort Worth has more than sixteen square miles of public parks. In Rock Springs Park are the municipal Botanic Gardens, rivaling Tyler's in their profusion.

An architectural adornment of considerable splendor is the new Casa Mañana, a circular theater under a gold-anodized aluminum dome in Amon Carter Square, for plays-in-the-round.

All in all, Fort Worth is an excellent city for people who want the benefits of urban life, but cherish their independence. More subdued than Dallas or Houston, more homespun than San Antonio or El Paso, it still offers the essential services and markets that draw an outdoor populace to the city in the first place, while it gives the effect of being simply an unusually elaborate roadside park on the plains.

Fort Worth no longer dominates the empty land to the west as it once did—primarily because the land no longer is as empty as it used to be. From its old-time identity as a cattle town, Fort Worth has fashioned a new and varied character of a different kind. Yet even now it has the tang of rawhide in its air, the lean flavor of beef in its marrow. Fort Worth—if not the West itself any more—still is where the West begins.

8: —the West Begins

**Turkeys on the Hardie Ranch
between May and Rising Star**

Fred Nobs

No startling change in the landscape, no abrupt alteration in climate, mark the beginning of West Texas. The plains roll on toward New Mexico, gradually rising, growing imperceptibly drier and more lonely. From about 700 feet on the outskirts of Fort Worth, the ground climbs in undulating waves to nearly 3,000 feet at Midland and Odessa, on the southern fringe of the Llano Estacado, the broad plateau beyond the plain.

The rainfall thins out with the same deliberation, from thirty-two inches a year at Fort Worth to half as much at Midland or Odessa, and half of that in El Paso. The air becomes noticeably cooler and clearer.

For the first hundred miles to the west, the terrain is a gentler version of the Hill Country. Vanishing forests of post oak alternate with meadows of sparse grama grass. This is farming country of a marginal variety. Cotton was tried long ago, and generally abandoned. But peanuts thrive in the rust-colored soil.

Before the long drought began in 1949, Comanche County, east of Brownwood, produced as much as forty million pounds of peanuts a year, and other neighboring counties were not far behind. By 1954, the crop had been cut to one-quarter, even though peanuts get along in arid soil. Now that the drought is over, they are coming back.

Municipal Park, San Angelo

Quincy Howe, Jr.

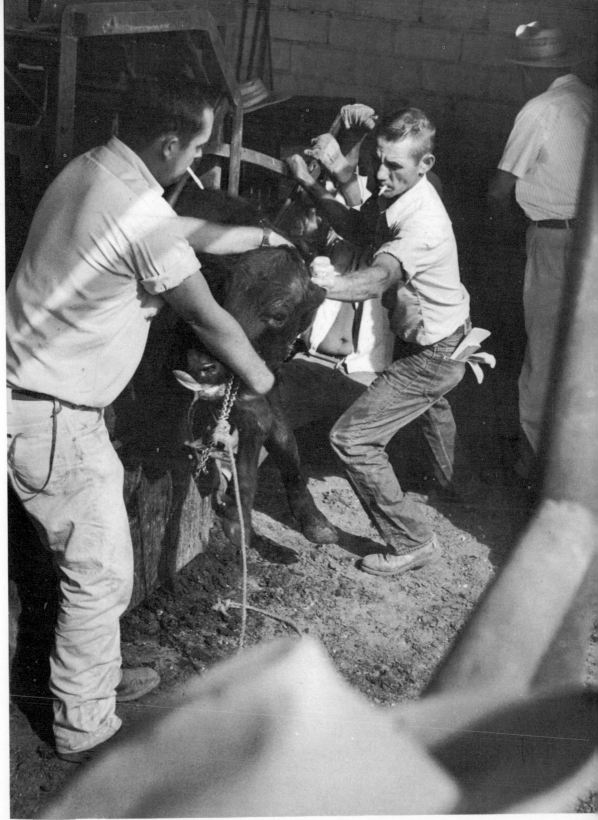

Quincy Howe, Jr.

Vaccinating steer in San Angelo Stockyards

In the same area, pecans not only grow wild along the rivers—as they do in other parts of Texas—but are grown as a crop in orchards, like apples or peaches in moister states. There is a Texas Pecan Growers' Association, with headquarters at A&M College, where scientific methods of cultivation are studied. New machines have been developed in the last few years to harvest pecans from the trees and gather them off the ground.

Before the drought, the annual harvest from pecan groves in San Saba County reached 800,000 pounds. Like the peanut crop, it was reduced by a succession of dry seasons, but is reviving. Other nearby counties have been turning from miscellaneous food crops to pecans.

Diversity is the rule along this borderland of the West. Scattered among the farms are small ranches, grazing cattle, sheep, or goats. This is also turkey country. San Saba, Eastland, and Erath Counties all had more than 100,000 turkeys in 1954, the worst year of the drought—though none matched the 137,000 gobblers in De Witt County, the turkey capital of South Texas.

The first city of any size between Fort Worth and the border of New Mexico is Abilene. It is a smaller, somewhat jauntier copy of Fort Worth, reflecting the variety of the activities around it. Like Fort Worth, too, it is an educational center. In Abilene is Hardin-Simmons University, one of the regional schools that have great prestige in Texas. Its athletes call themselves the Cowboys.

The Baptist Church sponsors Hardin-Simmons. Abilene Christian College—like Texas Christian in Fort Worth—belongs to the Disciples of Christ. The Methodist Church provides McMurry College.

The West Texas Chamber of Commerce makes its headquarters in Abilene. While no one city can be said to typify the vast extent of West Texas, Abilene might reasonably claim the title that Fort Worth wears. For here the wooded section of the plains—known technically as the Cross Timbers, running down from Oklahoma into the Hill Country—comes to an end, and the vacant reaches which are characteristic of the West begin in earnest.

One seemingly empty spot among those reaches soon will be somewhat less vacant than it looks. Near Dyess Air Force Base, outside of Abilene, is the site chosen for the only intercontinental ballistic missile base in Texas.

It will be what missile men call a "hard" base. That is, the launching platforms will be sunk in concrete silos 165 feet underground. Nothing will be visible above the plain except an apparently aimless hatchwork of highways, leading nowhere in particular.

The Dyess complex will conceal an augmented squadron of thirteen Atlas missiles, poised upright on their pads, ready for firing within about fifteen minutes after an alert. The crews will occupy separate caverns hollowed out of the earth. Tunnels will connect them with the silos, waiting silently for the command that could send the rockets out of their hidden shafts on billows of flame.

This will be the southernmost missile base in the United States. Its nearest companions will be at Altus, Oklahoma, 165 miles to the north, and at Walker Air Force Base, near Roswell, New Mexico, about 300 miles to the west.

A missile base is not an unalloyed blessing to the nearby community, despite the money it dispenses to merchants and contractors. Unlike a military airfield, a nest of long-range missiles serves no visible purpose in defending its neighbors from attack. On the contrary, its presence can draw attention to them, and make them a target for messengers of destruction from the other side of the world.

But Abilene is taking that possibility without dismay. If anything, it is proud to be the only Texas city capable of striking a blow for freedom, against an unseen enemy 5,000 or more miles away.

No more pointed contrast could be found to the space-age menace of the missile base than another public facility a few miles out of Abilene. In Fort Griffin State Park, near Albany, is one of the last two herds of Longhorn cattle remaining in Texas. The state supports it as a reminder of the past.

The Longhorn carried the burden of the old-time Texas cattle empire. It was an ornery, wild, and self-sufficient critter, descended from the fierce fighting cattle which the Spaniards brought to America in the sixteenth century. Lean and tough, it was in its own way as ominous as a ballistic missile.

A full-grown Longhorn weighed around 750 pounds. It was worth about ten or fifteen dollars to anybody who could find a way of getting it to a market. But it had the supreme virtue of being hardy. Like a missile, it could travel on its own momentum. So generations of Longhorns marched toward their own destruction the 750 miles or so to the nearest railhead, living on thin grass and occasional water along the way.

After the railroads arrived in Texas, cattlemen turned to less sinewy breeds with more meat on them, starting with the Hereford. Nearly all the beef cattle in Texas today belong to one of these domesticated types, including the Shorthorn, the Aberdeen-Angus, the Brahma from India, and the Santa Gertrudis, developed by the King Ranch on the Gulf Coast.

Central High School, San Angelo

A full-grown Hereford is twice as heavy as a Longhorn, and is worth five or six times as much. As a result, though the cattle population of Texas dropped from an all-time high of 9,500,000 in 1906 to about 7,735,000 half a century later, their value increased from $155,000,000 to about $510,000,000.

But Texans, visiting Fort Griffin Park, look on the rangy Longhorns there with much the same veneration as that felt by an aristocratic Briton when he surveys the portraits of his piratical ancestors. The Longhorn was mean, and lived by its strength and endurance. Yet it had a kind of class which is lacking in the sluggish purebred beasts of today.

South of Abilene about sixty-five miles, on the way to San Angelo, is another relic of the past in Texas. Outside the town of Paint Rock, on the Concho River, is a bluff with overhanging rock walls that once sheltered the nomadic Indians who followed the buffalo herds over the plains.

For more than half a mile along this rock gallery the Indians left their tribal records inscribed in painted picture symbols. More than 1,500 pictographs, well preserved in the dry air, describe events that seemed to the historians worthy of remembrance. Tourists have added their timeless touch by scrawling their initials over the paintings.

San Angelo belongs equally to the Hill Country and to the plains. A bit smaller than Abilene, with about 60,000 people, it is the primary market for sheep and goats, wool and mohair, in an immense territory reaching from Kerrville and Fredericksburg beyond the Pecos almost to El Paso.

The great event of San Angelo's year is the Stock Show and Rodeo in March, when herdsmen from all over West Texas congregate in its modern hotels and motor courts. The city also puts on a National Wool Pageant in August.

San Angelo was founded on the site of Fort Concho, one of the most famous frontier posts of the Army in the West. The remains of the old

Quincy Howe, Jr.

150 fort have been restored, and serve San Angelo as a civic center. Among other attractions, they house the West Texas Museum.

Although the Army departed with the Indians about seventy years ago, San Angelo still keeps a military guard on its outskirts. Goodfellow Air Force Base is a prime training center for airmen.

The importance of the city as a market has brought quite a few miscellaneous industrial activities to San Angelo. One of the most unusual is the five-mile test track of the Goodyear Tire & Rubber Company, on a circle of flat ground beyond the corporate limits.

Automobiles whine around the track incessantly, testing their treads at speeds up to 140 miles an hour. Among the peculiar problems that

A park in San Angelo

Quincy Howe, Jr.

Burvin Hines

Downtown Midland

Goodyear has to cope with in San Angelo is to keep teen-age drivers of hot rods from invading the track and staging impromptu races.

Another reason for the growth of industry in San Angelo in recent years is oil. San Angelo lies on the rim of an enormous pool of oil that reaches all the way into the southeast quarter of New Mexico.

The Permian Basin, as this underground sea of petroleum is known, includes more than a dozen separate fields of major proportions, and countless smaller ones. In the past decade it has transformed 60,000 square miles of West Texas from a tranquil pasture land into a jungle of storage tanks and derricks.

The whole thing began back in 1923, when a shallow well came in on the dry plain at Big Lake, about sixty miles west of San Angelo. (The lake is a brackish water hole that evaporates in the sun, without any outlet to the sea.) In the next few years, other fields were found from time to time at widely scattered points around Big Spring, Midland, and Odessa. But the great discovery by Dad Joiner in East Texas distracted attention from the isolated region in the West. Exploration went on in a leisurely way through the 1930's and 1940's, now and then adding some new production to the area.

The lid blew off in November 1948, with the uncovering of the fabulous Canyon Reef reservoir, near the town of Snyder in Scurry County. It spread into neighboring Borden and Howard Counties, and its discovery led within a year to the development of the world's richest oil-producing territory in the Permian Basin.

Two counties farther west, Andrews and Ector, stood at the top in Texas oil production in 1956, with sixty-four million and fifty-seven million barrels respectively. Scurry was No. 4, with over 42½ million barrels. The largest East Texas county in oil production (Gregg) by that time was only in third place.

The last time anybody counted, there were 77,618 active oil and gas wells in the Permian Basin. They poured out a total of nearly 543 million barrels in 1959. Altogether, they had given the nation almost eight billion barrels, and there still were proven reserves of more than seven billion barrels in the ground, with new discoveries coming in all the time.

Every large oil and gas producing company in the United States operates in this part of Texas. The ranking native firm is the Cosden Petroleum Corporation, with headquarters at Big Spring.

It would be almost impossible to exaggerate the effect that oil has had on this once nearly deserted region. Every town and hamlet has grown several times over, proliferating with modern highways, buildings, and industrial enterprises. Pipe lines, wells, and pumping stations weave their intricate geometrical patterns over the grasslands between the towns.

The chief cities in the basin are Odessa and Midland, just twenty miles apart on the edge of the High Plains, near the corner of New Mexico. Like Fort Worth and Dallas in miniature, they carry on a running feud— even down to the airport in Midland County, which they share without any enthusiasm whatever. Odessa is bigger and more active industrially. Midland is older, more polished, and wields more power.

In the broad expanse of ranch country around both cities, Midland was a modest banking and commercial center for half a century before the present boom. As long ago as 1910, Midland had about 2,000 inhabitants—which was a respectable population for that part of Texas at that time.

When oil turned up on the ranches, the owners naturally signed their leases and banked their royalties in Midland, as usual. By 1940 it had grown into an urbane community of more than 9,000 citizens. Today it has around 65,000.

Like Dallas on a considerably smaller scale, Midland specializes in finance and management. Its fifty-four office buildings—most of them new, and one of them the tallest between Fort Worth and El Paso— house the regional homes of more than 650 companies doing business in the oil fields. Midland's three banks do not begin to compete in resources with the mighty Republic National Bank in Dallas. But their combined

El Paso Natural Gas Company makes butadiene at Odessa

deposits, adding up to about $125,000,000, control the money market in this diocese of Texas.

As a city inhabited largely by financiers and executives, Midland boasts of the highest per capita income in the nation. The Petroleum Club of Midland is the most elegant resort west of Dallas. Two handsome country clubs adorn the bare plain around the city.

Moreover, Midland pays respectful attention to the arts. Irma Mancill's Book Stall does a flourishing business, and there is a spacious downtown library. Midland supports a small but excellent symphony orchestra and a community theater with its own modern playhouse.

Odessa was little more than a crossroads as late as 1920, when the whole of Ector County contained only 760 people. By 1940 its population already had passed Midland's, and today Odessa can count about 80,000 citizens.

154   Odessa is the functioning heart of the huge petroleum district that Midland manages. Its economy rests mainly on oil refineries, petro-chemical plants, and oil-field equipment companies. Not long ago, Odessa completed a $48,000,000 complex for the joint use of tire manu-facturers making rubber out of butadiene and styrene.

One of the pleasant things about oil in a ranch country is that sub-terranean drilling doesn't interfere too much with the peaceful grazing of animals above ground. For example, Midland County still supports nearly 22,000 head of cattle in the midst of its oil operations.

The old-time cattle families have found that their traditional in-fluence is waning in Midland, under the influx of oil administrators and engineers. But Odessa is bidding for their allegiance, with an annual Hereford and Quarterhorse Show and Rodeo.

Odessa also has two natural attractions for visitors that Midland—with all its money—can't match. Ten miles to the west, off the highway, is a great hole in the ground that makes the little pipes drilled by men look like pinpricks. It was left by the fall of a meteor many thousands of years ago.

The crater near Odessa is the second in size in the United States—after the phenomenal meteor crater in Arizona—and the fourth in the world. It measures 510 feet across. Originally more than 90 feet deep, it has filled up by erosion through the centuries, until its depth now is only about 15 feet. Bits of meteoric rock and metal, dug out of the crater, make pleasant souvenirs from space.

The second attraction is twenty miles or so farther on. It is a strip of white sand hills, resembling the Sahara, that crosses the highway near the town of Monahans, and reaches up into New Mexico.

Texas has set aside six square miles of this desert waste as a state park, complete with tourist quarters and an archeological museum. The sand hills—like the petroleum under them—are a relic of the prehistoric sea that covered the Permian Basin. They also remind the traveler that he is now truly in the West.

9: The High Plains

Howe, Jr.

A cattle ranch in the Panhandle

HE Texas Panhandle—that corridor running northward from the main body of Texas, in the general direction of the Arctic Circle—has been the subject of more jokes and less information than any other part of the state. The jokes usually deal with the weather, which has a tendency to be cold in winter and breezy at any season.

There's the one about the plainsman who was asked, "Does the wind blow this way all the time?"

"No," he said. "Sometimes it blows the other way."

Natives of the Panhandle (and it isn't considered funny to refer to them as Panhandlers) will tell you with a sort of perverse pride that there is no other place in the inhabited world where you can look farther and see less.

To an extent, this is true. The character of these North Texas plains is such that you can go a long way and not see anything much except an endless expanse of dry land, with an occasional windmill rising forlornly above it. There are few streams, and most of these are barely wet enough to moisten the ground lightly as they go by.

The Panhandle actually belongs to two separate regions. An irregular line of stony hills and bluffs—known as the Cap Rock—runs diagonally across it, from just below Odessa to the northeast corner, beyond the town of Canadian. It forms a natural terrace, broken by deep canyons, raising the level of the land as much as 1,000 feet.

At the foot of the escarpment are the dry prairies of Northwest Texas and Oklahoma, tenanted chiefly by cattle on a few great ranches. At the top of it are the High Plains of the West, ascending to the continental divide beyond the Pecos and the Rio Grande in New Mexico. They are even drier than the prairies to the east.

But their appearance is deceiving. In the last few years especially, the High Plains have developed into one of the most abundant regions in Texas. Their wealth is founded primarily on four products of nature: oil, cattle, wheat, and cotton. All of these, in the Panhandle, involve drilling holes in the ground, to tap the hidden treasures underneath it.

There are times when Divine Providence seems determined that every part of Texas shall be rich. The vagaries of weather and the earth's resources that keep one region from becoming too lordly bring prosperity to another. So it has been with the Panhandle.

156

Cotton in a field near Lubbock

Quincy Ho

At the precise moment when eight years of drought were beginning to cause other areas to tighten their belts, oil started to flow bountifully at the lower end of the Panhandle. And just as other sections were abandoning cotton for peanuts or calves, the Panhandle found a way of making it burst from the boll.

The secret was simple: dig more water wells. The High Plains had always drawn their water from underground. But they had pumped it sparingly, in quantities just sufficient for the farmer and his animals to drink.

Then all at once, as World War II ended, farmers in the Panhandle were seized by a well-digging fever. Perhaps it was caused by the fact that there were so many rigs around, drilling for oil. They used the water that gushed forth to grow cotton in irrigated fields.

In three years, from 1946 to 1949, cotton production in Lynn County, south of Lubbock, rocketed from 18,000 bales to more than 185,000 bales. In Hockley County, just west of Lubbock, it jumped from 20,000 to more than 200,000 bales. The same pattern was repeated in a wide crescent of counties on the High Plains around Lubbock.

Overnight, this fertile district became the cotton bowl of the nation, producing nearly a third of the white fiber grown in Texas (the No. 1 cotton state) and 11 per cent of all American cotton.

As a result of this transformation—paralleling the one that built Midland and Odessa into important cities—Lubbock since 1940 has expanded from a modest commercial center of 32,000 people into a busy cotton market of nearly 130,000 residents. On the northern rim of the Permian Basin, Lubbock also has benefited by the oil boom. It is today the second largest Texas city—after Amarillo—in the broad sweep of parched land between Fort Worth and El Paso.

Although its phenomenal growth has occurred along with the spectacular rise of Midland and Odessa—and partly from the same causes—Lubbock shows a decided contrast to the twin cities at the south end of the Panhandle.

Both Midland and Odessa look as if they had sprung up on the plains overnight, materializing out of invisible particles in the air. Midland is a cosmopolitan business capital in miniature, Odessa a modern industrial complex on a reduced scale, and neither gives any clear evidence of its origins.

Lubbock, on the contrary, was a substantial city—though a small one—when its vast increase began. New office buildings, lifting their aloof profiles on its skyline, stand alone among the traditional one-story structures of a western town.

160

Although it has entered the new era which is remodeling the face of Texas, Lubbock still clings to the homely atmosphere of an old-time farm-and-cattle market on the plains.

Along with cotton gins, cottonseed mills, and a host of random manufacturing plants, Lubbock is the site of the ranking educational institution in the Panhandle. Texas Technological College—with a student body surpassed in numbers only by the University of Texas and the University of Houston—lately received the supreme accolade of maturity in a Texas school. Its football teams were admitted to the mighty Southwest Conference.

A Lubbock monument of a more peculiar kind is Prairie Dog Town, in Mackenzie State Park, on the edge of the city. It is a haven for the scattered ranks of the excitable little rodent that once populated the plains in enormous numbers. As recently as 1901 the Department of Agriculture estimated that there were at least 400 million prairie dogs in Texas alone. One of their underground colonies was said to have reached for 250 miles in one direction and 100 to 150 in the other, covering an area of about 25,000 square miles—almost half the extent of the Permian Basin.

Prairie dogs live on the same grass, the same vegetables, seeds, and tubers that support men and their animals. Panhandle farmers and cattle ranchers exterminated the furry pests with poison, until no more than a few thousand remained. At that point Lubbock and the National Park Service stepped in to protect the survivors.

The 600 or so prairie dogs in Mackenzie State Park have turned out to be an important economic resource for Lubbock. With their inquisitive manners, their odd antics, and their canine bark, prairie dogs appeal to sightseers. The Lubbock colony is said to attract a million visitors a year from Texas, Oklahoma, and New Mexico.

The principal cities of the Panhandle—Lubbock, Amarillo, Plainview, Pampa, Borger—all are on the Llano Estacado, as the awed Spaniards christened the High Plains. But one of the most fascinating minor cities can be found at the foot of the Cap Rock, forty miles southeast of Lubbock.

Post came into being as an individual act of creation by a man with an urge to own a town. He was the late cereal magnate, C. W. Post, of Battle Creek, Michigan, founder of the packaged protein industry now known as the General Foods Corporation.

Post rode out on the virgin prairie one day in 1906 and bought three adjoining cattle ranches—covering about 300 square miles—in what is now Garza County. They cost him $700,000.

Howe, Jr.

At the foot of the Cap Rock

Natives wondered then, as they do now, what had put this odd idea in the cereal king's head. A puzzled cowhand asked Post's agent, "What on earth is he going to do with all this land?"

The agent said, "He's going to plow it up and plant Grape Nuts."

That wasn't exactly what Post did, but it was close. His original plan was to sell the land to farmers in neat parcels of 80 to 160 acres. He needed a county government to register the deeds, and in order to have a county he required a county seat. So he built the town of Post from scratch, hauling in lumber from Fort Worth, stone from a quarry in the Cap Rock, and a mason from Scotland.

Quincy H

On the High Plains

The town opened up for business on July 4, 1907. It consisted of one half-completed block of stores and offices—known as the Double U—a smaller building surmounted by a bell tower for alarms and proclamations, and a cottage for the owner and his friends.

Post had promised the citizens that he would bring a railroad in. According to his associates, it took another $50,000 to persuade the Sante Fe—but on May 5, 1911, the line went through, incidentally giving a rail connection to Lubbock, which was then a town of about 2,000 people.

Meanwhile, the land hadn't sold too well—mainly because Post felt that it was his moral duty to be businesslike in his dealings with the colony he had founded. He was asking up to $30 an acre for the grassland that had cost him $3.50 an acre.

As an inducement to farmers, Post built a cotton gin that went into operation in the fall of 1911. The next year he built the Postex Cotton Mill. It cost him $650,000.

Postex, much expanded, still makes cotton sheets and pillow cases. It is the main industry of Post today.

As early as 1912 there was talk of oil under Garza County. Post himself tried drilling a well. He abandoned it at 2,500 feet—just 600 feet above the Garza Field that came in on his property twenty years later.

The High Plains

In 1914, at the age of sixty, Post died, leaving the care of his town to his descendants. It would have pleased him had he known that one day Post would contain thirty-four producing oil wells inside the city limits, and that Garza County would rank sixtieth in oil production among the 254 counties of Texas.

North of Lubbock, on the High Plains, cotton gives way to wheat and cattle, the traditional products of the Panhandle. Here and there, however, in the sea of grass and grain, are islands that specialize profitably in other things.

Plainview, in a county blessed with cotton and wheat together, is also a dairy center—a considerable oddity in beef country, where a cow normally is either an animal for breeding purposes or a polite euphemism. The Panhandle Plains Dairy Show at Plainview in April used to be one of the great events of spring in the Panhandle. It languished because the small independent dairymen went back to grain and cotton. But large commercial dairy herds prosper around Plainview. Some thirty-seven grade-A establishments are scattered over the nearby country.

Both Plainview and the town of Hereford, southwest of Amarillo, are surrounded by irrigated farms growing garden crops and Irish potatoes. As it does elsewhere in the Panhandle, the water comes from subterranean stores that belong to the farmer, and doesn't have to be bought from a central irrigation district or authority.

Thanks to this advantage in production costs, and a region singularly free from pests, the truck farms of the central Panhandle can compete successfully with older areas in South Texas, California, and the East.

The truck gardens are something of an oddity too—especially for Hereford. Deaf Smith County, whose only populous community is Hereford, leads the Panhandle in both wheat and cattle. On the High Plains, the cattle business isn't as impressive as in other parts of Texas, because it takes so much more land to graze a single steer. At least eighteen other counties at intervals over the state have more cattle than Deaf Smith—starting wih Harris County, around Houston, which has almost twice as many.

The Panhandle became a range country, after the Civil War, simply because it offered vast stretches of available land. There seemed to be little likelihood then that anything except grass would ever grow on them. But with the spread of irrigation, from shafts deep in the ground, the range land is gradually being taken over by farms.

If the water holds out, a time may come when the High Plains—

164 once the home of such famous old-time ranches as the XIT and the Matador—will have no cattle left except dairy herds. The range will be overrun with lettuce and tomatoes.

Wheat is another matter. Winter wheat flourishes on the high, dry plains. It gives the Panhandle not only enough to feed Texas, but a surplus for export. Deaf Smith County harvests 1,500,000 bushels a year. A dozen other northern counties grow comparable crops.

The only trouble with wheat is that the whole nation produces far more than it needs. Any time the taxpayers get tired of paying storage costs on the balance, wheat growers on the High Plains might have to start thinking about lettuce and tomatoes too.

Another prospect that haunts the Panhandle, in the midst of its miraculous good fortune, is the gradual depletion of its water. Conservation experts say that the subterranean reservoir isn't really inexhaustible, as it seems—that the only source of water under the plains is the meager twenty inches of rain and snow that falls in an average year—that the hoard which the Panhandle is drawing up so lavishly from 40,000 or more wells is the accumulation of centuries, and can never be replaced.

If so, the era of unrestricted water use for irrigated crops may be coming to a close. The Midway Research Institute, near Plainview, already is trying to figure out ways to conserve water—or, better yet, to replace it in the caverns underground. Meanwhile the drought is over;

Texas Technological College, Lubbock

Quincy Howe, Jr.

Quincy Howe, Jr.

Grain elevator at Lubbock

Quincy Howe, Jr.

Garza County Courthouse, with statue of C. W. Post

the water table seems to be holding its own for the present; and the Panhandle is enjoying its prosperity, confident that man's ingenuity—or Divine Providence—will find a way to prolong it.

The center of the wheat and cattle country in the northern part of the Panhandle is Amarillo. There the same exuberant increase which has been at work elsewhere on the High Plains can be seen again—but with somewhat less urgency. One reason is that Amarillo started growing earlier.

For many years Amarillo was the business and financial capital of the Panhandle. Back in 1910, when Lubbock was a largeish town of 2,000 inhabitants, Amarillo was already a smallish city of 10,000. It has grown steadily over the years. With roughly 140,000 people today, it just manages to hold approximately the lead over Lubbock that it started with. Amarillo still is the business and financial capital of the Panhandle, occupying much the same place of eminence that Dallas holds in East Texas.

Oil turned up at Amarillo's end of the Panhandle as long ago as 1921, in three adjoining counties northeast of the city. Amarillo's field has never been either as vast or as rich in oil as the Permian Basin. Gray and Hutchinson Counties, where the greater part of the flow is found, rank twenty-first and twenty-second among the oil-producing counties of Texas. But the Northern Panhandle turned out to be one of the finest natural gas fields in the world.

Natural gas—which once was burned off as a waste product in the oil fields—is in many ways more versatile than oil. It lends itself to a variety of uses. It can be consumed on the spot by industrial plants, as an abundant ready-made fuel. It can be piped for great distances to other regions, where sources of fuel are meager. Or it can be converted into

Sorghum is a staple crop in the Panhandle

168

refined products like gasoline or butane, or into synthetic fibers, rubber, and plastics.

Amarillo has prospered by nearly all of these uses. Two of the major industries headquartered in Amarillo are the Shamrock Oil & Gas Corporation and the Southwestern Public Service Company, which turns gas into electric power, selling it in Texas, Oklahoma, and New Mexico.

A huge zinc smelter moved into Amarillo—hundreds of miles away from any zinc—because it is cheaper to haul the ore to the Panhandle than to convey vast quantities of fuel to the mines. On the other hand, pipe lines reach out from the gas fields around Amarillo to the West Coast, to Denver, to Chicago, and to New York City.

Amarillo has a virtual monopoly on one of the rare by-products of natural gas. At suburban Soncy and at Exell, thirty miles north of Amarillo, the United States government extracts helium from the gas.

Valued before World War II as a light, nonflammable substitute for hydrogen in dirigibles and balloons, helium now finds more vital uses in the production of atomic energy and in rocket missile operations. It may some day replace nitrogen as an inert gas in the cabin air provided for space travelers.

Nor does Amarillo neglect the cultural aspects of life. It has a symphony orchestra of professional quality. Its educational institutions

The Panhandle-Plains Museum at Canyon

Quincy Howe, Jr.

170   include Amarillo College and the Musical Arts Conservatory of West
Texas. Just twelve miles away, at Canyon, is West Texas State College.

Two industrial offshoots of Amarillo, in the heart of the oil and gas
fields, are Borger and Pampa, each with about 25,000 people. Borger
specializes in carbon-black production, synthetic rubber plants, and refineries. It looks a little bit like a toy Pittsburgh.

Pampa is more diversified, with chemical industries, grain elevators,
mills, and packing plants. It is an agricultural and livestock market for
the northeast corner of the Panhandle.

One advantage of living in Amarillo is the variety of the scenery
within reach of it. The only real river on this part of the High Plains is
the Canadian, flowing through a deep gorge a few miles north of Amarillo.
The town of Canadian, over toward the Oklahoma border, where the river
drops down off the plains and issues onto the prairie, is noted for its scenic
grandeur.

A few miles south of Amarillo is the rugged Palo Duro Canyon,
where the headwaters of the Red River cut their way down through the
Cap Rock. One of the largest of the Texas state parks is in Palo Duro
Canyon. In addition to a spacious lodge with picture windows, saddle
trails, and camping areas, the park provides a two-mile, narrow-gauge
scenic railway—the Palo Duro, Burlington & Sad Monkey—that winds
along the lower end of the cañon.

Buffalo Lake, southwest of Amarillo, is one of several nearby conservation areas, with facilities for boating, fishing, and hunting. While
the Llano Estacado certainly is not endowed with the most seductive landscape on this ingratiating planet, neither is it the drab wasteland that
people passing through or over it often suppose. What nature has neg-
lected to supply, man has created in the Panhandle.

10: Beyond the Pecos

cobee

Remains of old Fort Davis, with town in background

*I*F you want to see Texas more or less as it used to be—unspoiled by too much prosperity—the place to look for it is on the vast sweep of the Edwards Plateau, stretching 400 miles to the west from the Hill Country. In all this enormous reach of territory, covering an area larger than the State of Iowa, there is only one city of any size— El Paso—and that one is as far removed from the rest of Texas as it possibly could be.

Far West Texas has little oil and less water, few farms and almost no industry. It consists mainly of dry land, basking in the sun, bearing a wispy cover of grass on which cattle and sheep graze. This is country of the kind that people from other parts of the world usually have in mind when they think of Texas.

Heading toward El Paso after sundown

Lynwood Abram

Statue of Cristo Rey looks down on El Paso

Lynwood Abram

Cement plant in the cañon outside El Paso

Compressor station of El Paso Natural Gas Company

Beyond the Pecos

For a reasonable facsimile of the Old West, you might try Loving County, on the Pecos River where it comes down out of New Mexico. Some eighty miles to the west from Odessa, Loving was named for a pioneer Texas cattleman, Oliver Loving, who was one of the openers of the Goodnight-Loving Trail.

Not only is Loving the lonelist county in Texas, it has been identified by the Census Bureau as the least populous county in the United States. Its inhabitants have been growing fewer with the years. In 1960 the census counted 226 people in Loving County.

Bare though it is, the land supported twelve times that many cattle. The bovine population in 1954 consisted of 2,859 beef cattle and calves—and seven milk cows, presumably for the school children, of whom there were then about thirty. Most of the people—and all of the cattle—lived on Loving's nine ranches, each with an average of about fifty square miles. Simple arithmetic shows that it took roughly 100 acres of grazing land to raise one steer in Loving County.

In the northwest corner of the county, near the New Mexico line, a dam across the Pecos provides water for irrigation on a few small farms. The only highway runs across the southeast corner, to Mentone, the county seat.

With a 1960 census of 110 citizens, Mentone is the single urban community in Loving County. It contains a handful of stores, whose combined sales amount to maybe $50,000 a year, and the county offices. Except that there are no saloons, Mentone might serve as a model for a frontier town on television.

The Pecos is the second river in West Texas, the first being of course the Rio Grande. The Pecos flows down out of the Sangre de Cristo Mountains near Santa Fe, New Mexico, and joins the Great River not far from Langtry, where Judge Roy Bean declared himself the law west of the Pecos.

It divides the broad plateau neatly in half. The east side is a not-so-lofty extension of the High Plains in the Panhandle. On the west are scattered mountain ranges, rising abruptly out of the plain, that blend into the Sierra Madre Oriental of Mexico.

Perhaps because there is so little in West Texas except scenery, this is the great vacation land for Texans. Summer and winter, they strike out across the plains, to camp in the mountains beyond the Pecos, gaze at the weathered remains of old Army forts and stagecoach stations, and follow the trails of early travelers like Goodnight and Loving. Barren though the country looks to a casual passerby, it is rich in places of historic significance to those who live in Texas.

W. Ray Scott—National Park Concessions

Green Gulch entrance to the Chisos Mountains

178   At the little city of Pecos, a few miles down the river from Mentone, is one of the old crossings for men and cattle. (Goodnight and Loving forded the Pecos farther downstream, at Horsehead Crossing, where the Butterfield Overland Stage later went through on its way west.) Pecos now is on the main highway between Fort Worth and El Paso.

Here, in the summer of 1883, was held the first rodeo, an informal test of skill in riding, roping, and branding, among the hands of two competing cattle ranches. Although the rodeo has since become a big-time performance, with its climactic event of the year in New York City's Madison Square Garden, its origin still is celebrated at Pecos in July, where the West-of-the-Pecos Rodeo is somewhat closer in spirit to the first one.

Old Mission Church at Ysleta

Lynwood

Not far from Pecos, at the foot of the Davis Mountains, is a place formerly known as San Solomón Springs, where the stages stopped. The springs now supply water for irrigation to a newly developed and highly productive farming section around the modern towns of Balmorhea and Toyahdale.

In Balmorhea State Park, at Toyahdale, is an enormous outdoor swimming pool, fed by the springs. The whole of the Davis Mountains, to the south and west, is maintained by the state as a recreation area. A seventy-four-mile scenic highway circles through the hills around Mount Livermore, the second highest peak in Texas. Antelope, wolves, and coyotes inhabit the green valleys hidden away in the recesses behind their barren slopes. Golden eagles float lazily in the remote sky above them.

Fort Davis, at the entrance to this rugged region, is the most elevated town of any size in Texas. It stands nearly a mile up on the flanks of Blue Mountain. A few miles away, on Mount Locke, is the McDonald Observatory, operated jointly by the University of Texas and the University of Chicago. One of the most eminent astronomers in the nation, Dr. Gerard P. Kuiper, as Director of the McDonald Observatory, has conducted valuable studies of the solar system at its eighty-two-inch telescope, high in the clear air of the Davis Mountains.

The tallest individual peak in Texas is far to the north, on the border of New Mexico. Guadalupe Peak, 8,751 feet above the level of the Gulf, belongs to the Guadalupe Range that straggles northward in the direction of Alamogordo and the Mescalero Apache Reservation. Most of it is national forest.

Just across the line, in New Mexico, is the Carlsbad Caverns National Park, with its endless system of underground galleries. In the Diablo Mountains, forty miles or so to the southwest of the Guadalupe Range, is the last known herd of wild bighorn sheep. From here to El Paso, 100 miles away, there is little except empty land, too arid even for sheep, broken by one more isolated chain of mountains, the Huecos.

On this desolate expanse, in the shadow of the Huecos, is a development like nothing else in America. It consists of three phantom municipalities—Sun City, Horizon City, and Wilco Addition—with their imaginary suburbs, totaling 260 square miles of deserted rangeland, so far devoid of any human habitation.

These are not ghost towns in the ordinary sense. Instead they are populous towns yet unborn—mere figments in the minds of their begetters.

All three are strictly for speculation. Although vague plans have been drawn for a metropolis which is destined to be the future home of some 3,000,000 souls, reducing El Paso to the status of an outlying satellite, no promise has been made to build so much as an outhouse on the lots which are now being sold. Instead, the sites are offered by mail to investors over the country, on the assumption that mere ownership will enhance their value.

Horizon City is the handiwork of a real-estate corporation in Tucson, Arizona. Sun City belongs to a promoter in El Paso, Harlan O'Leary. His brother Gerald O'Leary is the developer of Wilco Addition. They have found buyers for at least 60,000 plots of ground around these non-existent communities, at prices ranging from $67.50 up to $737.50.

The nearest water is at least ten miles away, in rock formations deep underground. There isn't a vestige of industry or commerce nearer than El Paso, some thirty miles down a long slope dotted with occasional yucca trees. But land that was once almost as desolate, on the outskirts of that city, now supports tidy rows of ranch-style homes behind white picket fences. Nobody can say with absolute assurance that the environs of Horizon and Sun Cities won't some day do the same.

El Paso is the metropolis of a great, dry region all its own, encompassing Far West Texas, most of New Mexico, and the vast State of Chihuahua in northern Mexico. It belongs less to Texas than it does to that self-contained heart of the North American Continent.

El Paso has not escaped the growth which has expanded other Texas cities in the past two decades. But it draws the sustenance for its increase from other sources than the trade in its immediate environs.

Since 1940, El Paso has nearly trebled in size. It is now a city of more than 275,000 people. Juárez, a smaller reflection of El Paso on the Mexican side of the International Bridge (actually two bridges), has matched its rate of increase in population. Jointly they share something like 400,000 inhabitants, and form by far the most important center on the southern border of the United States.

Moreover, they behave as one entity. Citizens of both republics cross the river daily to work, to carry on their own affairs, or simply to enjoy themselves. More business flows into El Paso from the Mexican side of the Rio Grande than from West Texas and New Mexico together.

Although El Paso, as an American city, is barely a century old, it can make a good case for itself as the oldest community in Texas. As early as 1598, the Spaniards in Mexico began to travel by the site of Juárez and El Paso, on the way to their colonial outpost up the river, in the vicinity of Sante Fe.

The pass through the mountains which they called El Paso del

Casa Grande peak in the Chisos Mountains

Norte was the easiest route from Durango and Torreón to the territory in the far north. Not even the Indians lived there permanently then. According to Paul Horgan—the authoritative chronicler of the Great River —it was 1659 before the first mud church and straw-thatched monastery were built at the foot of the pass on the Mexican side, as a resting place for travelers.

An Indian revolt in 1680 drove the Spaniards out of Santa Fe. They fled down the river to the tiny settlement at what is now Juárez. On the opposite bank, reaching about fifteen miles downstream, they founded three missions known as Ysleta del Sur, Socorro, and San Elizario.

These were the first villages of European origin in Texas, thirty-eight years before the arrival of Don Martín de Alarcón in San Antonio. They were never more than drowsy islands of repose in the vast wilderness of plains and mountains enclosing them. But they became the nucleus of the present city of El Paso.

Until 1827 there was nothing else on the northeast side of the river. Then a Mexican rancher in Juárez, one José María Ponce de León, crossed over and built a new suburban villa. A few other householders from Juárez followed.

Their lives went on serenely in the valley of the Rio Grande, undisturbed by the brief war, 500 miles away, that made their land a part of the Texas Republic, or by the treaty, ten years later, that changed them into citizens of the United States. Their allegiance was to the bare slopes of the hills around them.

The California Gold Rush of 1849 opened El Paso to the world. It brought a train of 400 wagons, filled with emigrants following the trail of fortune, rumbling over the pass to the West. The stage lines rolled through in their wake.

Some of the fortune hunters tired of the journey, and stayed. An enterprising trader from Kentucky, James Wiley Magoffin, who had lived a number of years in Mexico, opened a store and a post office on the American side of the river. He called it Magoffinsville. Another village named Franklin came into being close by. On the eve of the Civil War, in 1859, they were merged into the town of El Paso.

As late as the year 1881—when the first railroad huffed into El Paso on the heels of the vanishing stagecoach—the city had less than 500 inhabitants. Since then, it has more than made up for lost time. By 1910 it had supplanted Galveston as the fifth city of Texas. It holds the same rank today, against the upsurge of municipalities like Austin, Corpus Christi, Lubbock, and Amarillo—all of them larger today than El Paso was only ten years ago.

El Paso is pre-eminently a city of services. It subsists less on its own resources than on what it does to the resources of the immense territory surrounding it. The strategic position of El Paso at one of the main cross-roads on the continent makes it an important transportation center.

Five rail lines converge on it from all directions. Two transcontinental systems—the Southern Pacific and a branch of the Santa Fe—enter on their own rails. The Southern Pacific yards are among the basic industries of the city. The Texas & Pacific and the Rock Island—using Southern Pacific tracks for the last few miles—link El Paso with the northern half of Texas and the Midwest. The National Railways of Mexico connect Juárez with all of Central America.

They bring in hordes of travelers, who stop long enough to visit Juárez, tour the bars and night clubs just across the bridge, buy curios and tequila in gaudy bottles, and attend the big Sunday afternoon *corridas* at the Plaza de Toros on Calle Abraham Gonzales. More than that, they bring in ores from the mines of northern Mexico, Arizona, Colorado, and New Mexico, to be processed in El Paso.

The Phelps-Dodge plant, on the eastern end of the city, is reputed to be the largest copper refinery in the world. The American Smelting & Refining Company rears the nation's tallest smokestack out of the cañon cut by the river through the hills to the west. It reduces tin, lead, and silver as well as copper ores. Water to run the smelters comes from Elephant Butte Lake, 125 miles up the Rio Grande in New Mexico.

El Paso has no oil or gas wells of its own, up to now. But it is the headquarters of a petroleum complex with the richest assets of any single enterprise in Texas. The El Paso Natural Gas Company owns property worth roughly one and a half billion dollars, consisting mostly of pipe lines reaching from West Texas and the Panhandle all the way to California, Oregon, and Washington. It also produces oil and gas in Texas, Canada, Venezuela, and the Gulf of Mexico.

El Paso Natural Gas ranked fourth in sales of all Texas companies in 1960. While many other businesses were suffering from the little recession, El Paso Natural Gas was one of a fortunate few that forged steadily ahead to higher earnings and more wealth for its stockholders. A very much smaller—but still substantial—El Paso company listed on the New York Exchange is Food Mart, Inc., a grocery chain.

El Paso's isolation makes it an important cattle market for the dry plains of West Texas, New Mexico, and Mexico. Like the environs of most Texas cities, El Paso County itself provides grazing room for cattle in considerable numbers on the bare slopes beyond its suburbs. Toward the end of the drought, in 1954, the only county in that part of Texas with a larger bovine population was Jeff Davis, down the river in the Big Bend country.

Even more valuable than cattle to El Paso is cotton. Its peculiar

Scott—National Park Concessions

Boquillas Village, Mexico, from Big Bend National Park

situation in the fertile Rio Grande valley, with access to water for irrigation, gives El Paso an advantage something like the one enjoyed by the Panhandle with its richly flowing wells. The cotton farms, bordering the river on both sides for sixty miles below El Paso, form a thin line of greenery between barren hills that looks something like the valley of the Nile.

And well it might. The cotton cultivated on this alluvial strip of soil is the same long-staple fiber grown in Egypt. It belongs to a variety called Pima, which the Rio Grande cotton growers have elaborated into a new term, Supima, to distinguish their own product.

The narrow band along the river brings in far less cotton than the High Plains. At its height in 1949, before the drought, El Paso's harvest was a little more than 100,000 bales. Lately it has been running around 80,000 bales—roughly a third of the crop in Lubbock County alone. But the fine quality of the staple makes up for its moderate yield. The value of the cotton crop to El Paso is somewhere in the neighborhood of $35,-000,000 a year.

The highway out of El Paso, to the south and east, runs beside these cotton farms until it passes old Fort Hancock, one of the many long-abandoned Army posts that once guarded the stage routes to the West. Then it swings eastward through the mountains, toward Sierra Blanca and Van Horn. It turns away from the river at this point, because here the rugged crests of the cordillera come down to the water. The valley narrows, and the Rio Grande plunges into the series of desolate cañons that carry it on its wide sweep around the Big Bend.

This is the only thoroughfare that crosses Texas from El Paso. At Van Horn the road divides. One branch goes on in the direction of Fort Worth and Dallas. The other heads southeast toward Del Rio, San Antonio, and eventually Corpus Christi and Brownsville. It skirts the western foothills of the Davis Mountains on its way into Marfa, Alpine, and Marathon.

Marfa is the seat of Presidio County, and its only town of any size. The county consists almost entirely of mountains, with a few large cattle ranches scattered through the valleys between them. The Army of the era before World War II remembers Marfa as the site of Fort D. A. Russell, the last home of the famed First Cavalry Regiment before it was mounted on wheels. The fort is now privately owned.

Alpine is the administrative center of Brewster County, the largest and one of the least crowded in the nation. The 6,208 square miles of Brewster County would contain both Connecticut and Rhode Island, with

Howe, Jr.

Rancher Bernard Petty with Suffolk sheep

Highway bridge over the Pecos, north of Del Rio

room to rattle around in. Its 6,500 people, or thereabouts, would fall a bit short of filling the Connecticut town of New Canaan. Most of them live in Alpine, which has among its attractions the excellent teaching facilities of Sul Ross State College.

Marathon is notable chiefly as the starting point of the highway that winds southward forty miles through the mountains to the main entrance of Big Bend National Park. Like almost all Texas highways, the road is as urbane as the driveway leading to a baronial estate, in spite of the lonely land that it traverses.

But it conveys the traveler to the wildest and least visited domain among the public preserves of the United States. Big Bend is just about the last view of the North American continent, in something resembling its pristine state, within our increasingly constricted borders.

The rough-hewn character of the park's terrain, and the fact that it was on no familiar track through the wilderness, kept it from being invaded by sightseers until a few years ago. The Apaches passed through it on their way to Mexico, over one difficult trail that led down to a ford across the Rio Grande. Wagon trains went by it at a safe distance, on the present route through Alpine and Marfa.

A U.S. Geological Survey team, in 1899, followed the winding channel of the river on its course through the cañons from Presidio to a point where it approaches the highway again, between Sanderson and Del Rio. But the interior remained largely unexplored until the modern development of Texas began around 1930.

The Legislature established Texas Canyons State Park in 1933, with the idea of offering it to the Federal government as the nucleus of a larger national park. The Congress of the United States authorized the acquisition of the Big Bend two years later, but it was 1941 before $1,500,000 was appropriated to pay for it, and purchase of the land began.

In 1944 the park was finally opened. Since then visitors have gone to see it in increasing numbers. But the great majority of them still are Texans, looking for the past of their own Republic. Big Bend is the only National Park in Texas.

It covers more than 1,000 square miles of mountains and desert, surrounding the intricate Chisos Range—the barrier that causes the Rio Grande to turn southward again and search for a circuitous passage toward the sea. The park begins on the west side at Santa Elena Canyon, a fifteen-mile gorge through the Mesa de Anguila, with sheer rock walls looming 1,800 feet above it. The river runs on through inaccessible Mariscal Canyon, and turns north into Boquillas Canyon, another great gorge twenty-five miles long at the eastern end of the park.

There is an atmosphere of solitude and grandeur in Big Bend National Park. The very name of the Chisos Mountains is said to be derived from the Spanish word *hechizo,* meaning "enchanted" or "bewitched." Although a paved road fifty-five miles long circles around the north side of the range, from the foot of Santa Elena Canyon to a camp site looking down across the river on the remote Mexican village of Boquillas, most of the park can be seen only on horseback or on foot, over hushed mountain trails. The Park Service provides cottages, supplies, and a post office at The Basin, a bowl in the hills by the Chisos.

From its mile-high isolation in the Big Bend, the land slopes down onto the wide expanse of the Edwards Plateau, a mere 2,000 feet or so above the sea. Between Presidio and Langtry, where Judge Roy Bean held court, the Rio Grande drops almost a quarter of a mile as it careens through the shadowy cañons. Just beyond Langtry it meets the Pecos, issuing out of a gorge traversed by the loftiest highway bridge in Texas.

This is sheep country. Before the drought Val Verde County around Del Rio grazed about 600,000 sheep, and sheared some three million pounds of wool each year. Neighboring counties were not far behind. Del Rio is their market, as the flocks.multiply again.

Del Rio is a much diminished copy of El Paso, relying almost entirely on agriculture. In Villa Acuña, across the river, it has a much diminished copy of Juárez, with bars and cabarets, curio shops, and a flourishing bull ring.

In fact, Del Rio belongs less to the plains and mountains of West Texas than it does to the hot brush country along the Mexican border. Del Rio is the beginning of another unique Texas phenomenon, the Lower Rio Grande Valley, near the Gulf.

11: Down in the Valley

Palms line the highway into Brownsville

Quincy Howe, Jr.

SOUTH and east of Del Rio, the land that borders on the Rio Grande is as different as it very well could be from the domain of El Paso. The bare plains and austere mountains give way to a succession of low hills, leveling out toward the Gulf. This is the region known to the Spaniards as the Chaparral (oak forest) or the Monte (woods), and to Texans as the Brush Country.

The hinterland is covered by dense thickets of mesquite, dwarf oak, prickly pear, and thorny shrubs. The river valley, for the last 125 miles or so to the sea, is lined with palms, banana trees, orange groves, lush vegetable gardens, cotton fields, and tropical flowers.

South Texas is the area celebrated by Frank Dobie—a native of that section—in his early books, *A Vaquero of the Brush Country, Coronado's Children,* and *Tongues of the Monte.* It is a truly international territory, inhabited impartially—if not always equally—by Mexicans and Yanquís.

The Rio Grande, nearing the end of its 1,885-mile journey from the highlands of Colorado, is little more than a shallow creek as it saunters by Laredo, Reynosa, Brownsville, and Matamoros. Most of its water has been drawn off by irrigation, and much of the rest has evaporated under the inexorable sun that follows its course. People on both sides normally ignore it, traveling back and forth across the boundary as they please.

In its own peculiar way, this part of Texas is as much a wilderness as the expanse west of the Pecos. From the Nueces River, which trickles down off the Edwards Plateau a few miles out of Del Rio, and runs generally eastward in the direction of Corpus Christi, there are no regularly flowing streams of any kind all the way to the Rio Grande. As in West Texas and the Panhandle, ranchers collect water for their cattle in "tanks" —earthen reservoirs—from wells and springs.

The dry Monte is the natural home of rattlesnakes, coyotes, and javelina, the fierce wild hogs of the Brush Country that Texans hunt for sport. Its most familiar bird—next to the watchful vulture—is a speedy little creature that Mexicans call a *paisano,* because it looks like a ragged peasant, and Texans a chaparral bird or roadrunner, because it races along the highway on foot like a chicken, instead of flying.

Except for cattle and a small amount of oil, practically nothing is produced in the Monte. It is one of the world's most bizarre deserts—a sandy waste simmering under a cloak of useless vegetation.

Down in the Valley

More than a century ago, the Monte was a grassland, interspersed by head-high forests of scrub oak. That was when the Spaniards named it the Chaparral—from which came the word "chaps," to describe the leather leggings or *chaparejos* worn by vaqueros on horseback, chasing steers through the brush.

Cattle brought the tough mesquite bean north out of Mexico, leaving undigested kernels in their droppings along the way. Mesquite took over the grass and the forest alike. Its crooked, spine-covered branches have usurped the Chaparral, and turned it into the Monte. Even bulldozers have a hard time clearing away the tangle of mesquite.

The productive areas of South Texas are on the fringe of the Brush Country—along the Gulf Coast, in the Lower Rio Grande Valley, and among the web of creeks and rivers that join the Nueces to the north. One of these fertile places is a small crescent of irrigated farms, known as the Winter Garden.

Lomita Mission at the city of Mission

Ken Snyder

194   This patch of greenery follows the curve of the Nueces as it comes down off the plateau and turns toward the Gulf. It starts at Uvalde, midway between Del Rio and San Antonio, and ends at Cotulla, midway between San Antonio and Laredo.

Uvalde is the home of John Nance Garner, the noncommittal Texan who was Vice-President of the United States for eight rousing years while the President was Franklin D. Roosevelt. Now in his nineties, Garner is as uncommunicative as ever about the historic New Deal Era which he helped to inaugurate—not always, it was said, with whole-hearted enthusiasm.

Once every year, in November, Uvalde enjoys a day of national attention as a dateline in the press, when reporters interview the cryptic sage on his birthday. Among the guests who celebrated Garner's ninetieth anniversary, in 1958, were Senator Lyndon Johnson, Speaker Sam Rayburn (whose office Garner once held), and former President Harry Truman.

An irrigated field near Brownsville

Quincy H

Laredo on the Rio Grande

For the rest of the year, Uvalde is a somnolent city of some 12,000 farmers and ranchers, basking at the foot of the Balcones Escarpment. No less than a dozen minor offshoots of the Nueces start in the neighborhood of Uvalde, and the county bubbles over with cool springs, flowing into shady cañons.

Uvalde is famous throughout Texas for its honey, gathered by bees from the savory blossoms of the huajillo tree, a distant relative of the mimosa.

The market centers for the Winter Garden are Crystal City and Carrizo Springs, south of Uvalde in a section rarely visited by travelers. Both are packaging and shipping points for truckloads of winter onions, lettuce, corn and spinach, carrots, eggplant, squash, cantaloupes, and peppers, among other succulent vegetables. Little of the produce from the Winter Garden is ever eaten by Texans. Nearly all of it goes to the East, to be served on the tables of city dwellers who never heard of Dimmit or Zavala County, Texas.

The Brush Country is the only part of Texas which has lived under a genuine political dictatorship for a goodly number of years. Its long-

A church in Laredo

Quincy Howe, Jr.

time capital was the neat little city of San Diego, in Duval County, at the geographical center of South Texas. Its ruling dynasty was founded by the late Archer Parr, and was carried on for three decades by his son George Parr. In grudging tribute to their power, they were known far and wide as the Dukes of Duval.

The basic condition which made their reign possible is the biracial character of the Monte's people. South Texas was a preserve of Spanish and Mexican *rancheros,* before the Anglo-Americans moved in and took it over—sometimes by purchase, sometimes by force, and often by a little of both. The Latins stayed on as cowhands, workmen, and servants. Over the years they multiplied by constant immigration from Mexico— most of it surreptitious and unblessed by any authority on either side of the border.

Like immigrants everywhere, they were exploited. Largely illiterate, speaking little or no English on their arrival, they were ignorant of their rights and unable to make their numbers felt. Usually without entry papers, they looked for no protection from the law.

More than half a century ago, Archie Parr saw that he could turn the plight of the untutored Latins in Duval County to his own advantage —and incidentally to theirs as well. He took their side against the high-handed Anglo ranchers, herded them to the polls, and told them how to vote. In short, he became that hallowed figure of Central American politics, the *patrón* or *jefe.*

The elder Parr was satisfied with twenty years in the State Senate and the homage of his subjects. But George Parr, when he inherited the duchy, had visions of broader horizons. By manipulating the vote from the Brush Country in close elections, he saw a way to extend his influence over the state—and possibly even to Washington.

It was George Parr's portfolio of negotiable ballots that defeated Representative Richard Kleberg of the King Ranch Klebergs back in the 1930's, unseating the Congressman who had first introduced Lyndon Johnson to national politics.

Then a last-minute shift in the returns from Parr's district in 1948 sent Johnson to the United States Senate, with a state-wide margin of just eighty-seven votes over former Governor Coke Stevenson. An outraged cry of "Fraud!" arose from Stevenson's camp. Nothing came of it then, but the sharp scrutiny of state and federal authorities was turned on the Duchy of Duval.

A grand jury investigated Parr's activities. The Texas Rangers moved into Duval County. The federal government looked into the

198   Duke's income-tax returns. A Parr opponent was mysteriously murdered. There followed a long series of complicated indictments, arrests, trials, and appeals, culminating in January 1957, when Parr was convicted of appropriating public funds, given a five-year term in prison, and declared a bankrupt.

He was able to put off serving his sentence—perhaps indefinitely—with the help of his defender, Percy Foreman, one of the most colorful and astute criminal lawyers in Texas. But the power of the Parr dynasty was broken. Nothing could restore it again.

At the height of his dominion, back in 1945, George Parr bought the old Dobie Ranch. Covering eighty-seven square miles in the Brush Country northeast of Laredo, it had belonged to an uncle of Frank Dobie, and it was there that the author of *The Longhorns* had grown up.

San Ygnacio from the shade of the old Jesús Treviño House

Ke

The ranch was said to have cost Parr $422,000—at about $7.50 an acre—and he was credited with having put another $200,000 into improvements on it. At the long white ranch house, a few miles from the town of Freer, the Duke used to hold court with his henchmen in the days of his greatness.

On the steps of the Duval County Courthouse, in November 1960, the Dobie Ranch was auctioned off to satisfy a $662,000 judgement by the county against Parr, and to settle his other debts. The minimum bid was set at a million dollars. A seventy-three-year-old cattleman from Laredo, J. O. Walker, won the auction with a high bid of $1,575,000 in cash. That was the last vicarious gesture of munificence by George Parr.

The kind of personal patronage that Parr represented had already become an anachronism in South Texas. The *Latino* of today is reasonably well educated, familiar with his legal rights, and knows how to exert his influence at the polls. The Parrs had a good deal to do with his emergence from feudalism, whatever may be said about their methods. But an even more important factor has been the increasing prosperity of South Texas as a whole.

Duval County sits on the edge of a rich coastal petroleum area. After Nueces County, which encircles the port city of Corpus Christi, and Jim Wells County, its neighbor to the east, Duval itself ranks third in oil production in South Texas. The Parrs' own former stronghold, San Diego, touches the border of Jim Wells County, and is of some consequence as a service center for the oil fields. The counties to the south and west of Duval likewise produce oil in respectable quantities. So would the heart of the Monte, no doubt, if the mesquite didn't make exploration and drilling so troublesome.

Duval is crisscrossed by major highways, leading from Houston and Corpus Christi to Laredo, from San Antonio to the Lower Valley. All these influences contribute to its commerce, and to the relative sophistication of its present-day citizens. The Mexican border, with its brisk trade and international flavor, is only an hour or so away by car.

Laredo is of course the main port of entry between the United States and Mexico. Local traffic across the border is considerable, farther down the river. But nearly all the travelers and freight passing through Texas to or from the neighboring republic go by way of Laredo. The movement isn't only in one direction, by any means.

Northbound trucks and freight cars bring fresh produce, coffee, cattle, ores, chemicals, and building materials out of Mexico. Import duties on these cargoes provide the U. S. Customs at Laredo with about

$4,000,000 a year. Heading the other way, they carry tobacco, barley, drilling equipment, automobile parts, electrical appliances, and machinery.

This exchange of goods and people gives Laredo the character of an outlying diplomatic post—like Cairo or Tangier in other days. More than most Texas cities, it concerns itself with international affairs. Rumors collect there, and are passed on to the pilgrims proceeding over the bridge.

The ceaseless flow of traffic between the interior of Mexico and the interior of the United States, reaching back for more than 200 years, is the prime reason for Laredo's existence—and also for the existence of Nuevo Laredo, across the river.

The spot chosen for the crossing has almost no economic importance on its own account. There are no great tracts of irrigated farms and orchards on either side, as there are downstream, in the Lower Valley. For seventy miles or more in all directions, the land surrounding both Laredos is an arid waste of brush and desert.

But this is the midpoint on the most direct route between San Antonio and Monterrey, the great industrial center of Northern Mexico. Its geographical convenience has built Laredo into a city of at least 60,000 people, and Nuevo Laredo into one of perhaps 40,000. The inhabitants of both cities consist largely of freight-handling specialists, business and insurance agents, and government officials.

From Del Rio to Laredo and beyond, no streams of any size add their flow to the sluggish Rio Grande. But near Zapata, fifty miles below Laredo, the Río Salado drops down out of the Sierra Madre, bringing rain from the mountains of Coahuila, and restores the river to something resembling a respectable source of moisture. There is where the Lower Valley can be said to begin.

Between Laredo and Zapata, the only place that could be called a town, on either bank of the river, is the 200-year-old village of San Ygnacio, on the Texas side. It is a collection of sunbaked stone and adobe houses—one of them still occupied by the descendants of Jesús Treviño, who built it in 1767. Below Zapata, the towns become more frequent, and look as if they were built just yesterday.

In fact, they *were* built within the last decade. Zapata itself, Lopeno, and Falcon on the Texas side, and Nuevo Guerrero on the Mexican side, all were erected by the governments of the United States and Mexico. They were created to house people whose homes and shops and public buildings were submerged under the waters of Falcon Reservoir, a mammoth new lake stretching along the river for forty miles south of San Ygnacio.

Mexican picking oranges

ton trucks near Edna

Humble Oil & Refining Company

Humble Oil & Refining Company   *Humble Oil & Refining Company*

**Children salvage spilled
cotton near Harlingen**

La Sal de Rey, abandoned salt works near Edinburg

The reservoir was a joint project of the two governments. Completed in 1955 at a cost of more than $50,000,000, it holds back the turbulent winter floods that used to race down the Rio Grande, and provides the Valley with more water for irrigation. The lake covers about 175 square miles of brushland, bordering what was once the silvery thread of the river. Falcon Dam stretches for five miles between the low hills on either side.

A rickety toll bridge spanned the Rio Grande at Zapata. From the Mexican bank, a tortuous dirt road led to the town of Guerrero, at the mouth of the Río Salado. The bridge is now under fifty feet of water. Fish lurk on the cobblestone streets of the town, and dart through the faded pink arches of the Church of Our Lady of Refuge.

Guerrero was abandoned altogether and rebuilt twenty miles downstream. It is a modern city at the end of an asphalt highway that runs across the top of the dam.

Zapata, Lopeno, and Falcon were replaced by new towns three to five miles inland from their former sites. With them went their cemeteries, their crumbling municipal records, and the treasured artifacts of their citizens. The old buildings now stand empty in the uncertain depths of the lake. The new ones have an air of impermanence, as if they had been put up for a celebration, and might be dismantled and carried away tomorrow.

A few miles below the dam, the Rio Grande swings again to the east, on the last leg of its long journey to the Gulf. The towns become larger and more numerous on both sides of the river. A handsome toll bridge connects the adjacent Texas cities of Roma and Los Saenz (they

Down in the Valley

operate jointly but keep separate post offices) with the Mexican cities of Mier and Miguel Alemán. A ferry runs between Rio Grande City and Camargo.

Along this part of the river the fields on the Mexican shore are watered with more generosity than those on the Texas bank. Like the Río Salado above the dam, the Río San Juan comes down out of the Sierra Madre. The Mexican government has laid a dam across it, just before it reaches the Rio Grande. The huge El Azúcar Reservoir spills over plentifully onto the irrigated farms around it, while the Texas area across the way depends more on cattle, oil, and trade. Starr County is not very far behind Duval in petroleum.

As an economic and social entity, the Lower Valley starts on the outskirts of Mission, a half-hour's ride beyond Rio Grande City. From here to Mercedes, thirty miles away, it is no longer possible to distinguish between the cities. The boundary of one merges into the corporate limits of the next. They form a band of populous communities paralleling the river, each with its own shopping district—a kind of suburban complex without any metropolitan center attached to it.

On this thirty-mile-long Main Street are, besides Mission and Mercedes, the cities of McAllen, Pharr, San Juan, Alamo, Donna, and Weslaco. With Edinburg and several smaller towns on the edge of the strip, they share a population of at least 150,000, composed largely of people

Quincy Howe, Jr.

A church in Brownsville

whose occupation is farming. Nowhere else in the world, probably, is agriculture blended so agreeably with the amenities of urban life.

Over another toll bridge, near McAllen, is the Mexican city of Reynosa. Except for the fact that it has a little more Latin charm, Reynosa might very well be mistaken for one of the larger Texas cities.

The spectacular development of the Lower Valley was founded on its subtropical climate, which favors the growth of citrus fruits. Around 1750, the first orange grove in Texas was planted by Spaniards on the Laguna Seca Ranch, near what is now Mission. For almost two centuries oranges were cultivated in the valley on a modest scale, mostly for home consumption.

Then came the mighty boom in vitamins that followed World War I. Valley growers went into the production of grapefruit and oranges in a big way, and started shipping them to winter markets in the East.

From a few hundred thousand boxes in the early 1920's, the grapefruit crop kept mounting until it passed twenty-five million boxes—almost half the grapefruit grown in the United States—during the winter of 1946-47. The harvest of oranges expanded too, though not on quite the same grandiose scale.

The bane of Texas weather is the blue norther that comes whistling down off the plains of Wyoming and Montana in winter, reaching sometimes deep into Mexico. On January 25, 1949, one of the worst northers in the annals of Texas swept into the Valley. It left three-fourths of the citrus crop shriveled on bare and lifeless branches.

A newly planted grapefruit tree takes five or six years to attain its full production. The Valley citrus growers were just beginning to nurse their groves back toward maturity in February 1951, when two more hard northers struck in swift succession. This time the citrus crop was left virtually extinct. For the past ten years, it has been slowly coming back to life.

Losing so many of its citrus trees was a severe shock to the Valley. Yet it hasn't noticeably retarded the area's progress. While the new generation was maturing, citrus growers turned to other crops—mainly winter vegetables and cotton. Hidalgo County ranks first in Texas in garden produce, and just behind the two top Panhandle counties (Lubbock and Hale) in cotton.

Agriculture in this part of the Valley is almost a year-round activity. The growing season lasts 329 days, skipping only the month of January, and Hidalgo County can make four crops a year without putting forth any undue effort. Its canneries and frozen-food plants ship several hundred carloads north each week, by rail and truck.

Howe, Jr.

A Brownsville garden

The Valley has long been the scene of a real-estate promotion rivaling Florida's at its best. Its appeal has been directed largely toward elderly couples from the farming regions of the Midwest. If they had a little money saved, and felt like retiring to a sunnier climate, they would be invited to put their nest-egg into a citrus orchard, where they could earn a comfortable living without having to do any serious work.

Many of these retired couples found themselves in desperate straits after the 1951 freeze wiped out their citrus groves. But farmers are inured to the whimsies of the weather. Bankers in McAllen, Weslaco, Pharr, and Edinburg know that the Valley's prosperity depends on agriculture, and were as sympathetic as the Texas banking laws would let them be.

The elder folk survived somehow, and the real-estate campaign forges ahead as briskly as ever. It is spurred on by the fact that Hidalgo County's irrigated land is confined to the strip along the river, and already supports a sizable population. Falcon Reservoir has lengthened it a little, but the room for development still is limited.

The boom city of the Valley is Harlingen, just over the line a few miles from Mercedes, in Cameron County. Though its physical boundaries blend into the string of cities along the Rio Grande, Harlingen isn't really one of them. Its roots are in industry and trade, rather than agriculture. It belongs to the billowing maritime region on the Gulf Coast.

Half a century ago, when Mercedes was the only incorporated town in the present Rio Grande strip, Harlingen wasn't even marked on the map. Brownsville, about twenty-five miles to the south and east, was the sole city of any size at all in the Valley. Whatever agriculture there was along the river depended on Brownsville as a market.

Harlingen came into existence as an outlying suburb of Brownsville on the railway line to Houston. It grew modestly with the Valley's cotton and citrus crops. By 1940, Harlingen had about 13,000 inhabitants. Most of them were busy canning and shipping food or ginning cotton.

What changed Harlingen's outlook was the extension of the Intracoastal Canal from Corpus Christi to Brownsville in 1949, through the sheltered Laguna Madre that separates the South Texas mainland from Padre Island and the Gulf. A shallow bayou twenty-five miles long, known as the Arroyo Colorado, was all that stood between Harlingen and the Laguna Madre.

Following the example of Houston and other landlocked Texas cities which have dug channels to the sea, Harlingen persuaded the Army Corps of Engineers to dredge an offshoot of the canal through the Arroyo. Not only did it give Harlingen access to the low-cost barge traffic that plies the inland waterways of the United States; also it provided another port for shrimp boats, where they could put in to have their catch frozen and packed for shipment to far-off places.

Since then, Harlingen has blossomed into a city of some 40,000 souls, not far behind Brownsville itself. Its industries include machinery for food processing, oil supplies, and the inevitable chemical plants. Although Cameron County's oil production is negligible, Harlingen is a servicing and shipping point for Willacy County, to the north.

It is also a favorite spot for winter visitors in the Valley. From Harlingen, in thirty minutes or less, they can reach the garden cities on the Rio Grande, or Padre Island's level beach by the new causeway from

Nets drying on a shrimp boat

208

Port Isabel, or Brownsville with its toll bridge across the river to Mata-moros, where roads branch out to Monterrey, Tampico, and Mexico City.

There is little likelihood that Harlingen will overtake Brownsville in its heady rise to industrial importance. For one thing, Brownsville was there first, and is growing too, though not as fast as Harlingen and the other Valley cities. For another, Brownsville, like Laredo, is a center of international trade with Mexico.

Pan American and Eastern Air Lines, among others, stop at Browns-ville on their way to and from Central America. More than that, Browns-ville is both an inland-waterway and a deep-sea port. Cargo ships from Europe and the Mediterranean—as well as Mexico and the Caribbean—touch there.

Despite the fact that Brownsville is only thirty miles from the mouth of the Rio Grande at Boca Chica, its port is an artificial one like Hous-ton's. Even here at its end, the river is much too shallow for ocean-going vessels. Instead, Brownsville has cut a channel across the tongue of land that separates it from the south end of the Laguna Madre. Its harbor con-sists of a series of basins at the end of the channel.

Brownsville is the smallest of the major ports on the Texas coast. With its neighbor, Port Isabel, at the entrance to the channel, it handled

Shrimp boats on the beach at Port Isabel

Quincy How

a million and a half tons of shipping in 1959. One-third of its commerce was with countries abroad. The principal export from the Valley is cotton. Brownsville, in fact, is the leading cotton port of Texas and the nation. Domestic shipments are mainly of oil and chemicals.

A section of the Brownsville harbor all to itself is reserved for shrimp boats. The largest fleet of trawlers on the coast is based at Brownsville. They fish mostly off the desolate expanse of beach, 260 miles long, reaching southward from Brownsville to Tampico. On all that stretch of sand, the only inhabited place of any kind is the tiny Mexican fishing village of Soto la Marina.

The best trawling for shrimp is in shallow water, not very far offshore. But the coastal shelf narrows toward Tampico. The bottom drops away steeply toward the Sigsbee Deep, 2½ miles down.

Texas claims its territorial waters out to a distance of 10½ miles. Mexico asserts the same historic right. The United States defends a three-mile limit. The trawlers fish wherever they find shrimp.

Periodically they are intercepted by a Mexican gunboat and hauled into Tampico. The catch is confiscated, and fines up to 5,000 pesos (about $400) are levied against the owners. In Washington, Congressman Joe Kilgore's telephone jangles. The State Department expresses concern. The trawlers pay their fines and head glumly back to port.

The waters around Port Isabel teem with hardier creatures than shrimp. Some of the finest game fishing in the world is found at this end of the Gulf. Tarpon, sailfish, marlin, and barracuda abound in the open sea beyond Brazos Santiago Pass. Off the somnolent coast near Tampico, turtles the size of a small cabin cruiser have been seen drifting in the gray-green swells.

Every year, in August, Port Isabel puts on a three-day International Fishing Tournament. Recognized by the International Game Fish Association, it attracts marine sportsmen from all over the country.

Since the new causeway was built from Port Isabel to the southern tip of Padre Island, Cameron County has spent something like a million dollars to develop that once-deserted spit of land as a beach resort.

Isla Blanca Park, on the island, provides cottages and cabañas, a bath house, and a restaurant for vacationers. Outside the park, motor courts, a hotel, shops, and real-estate offices are preparing for the influx that Port Isabel expects when word of its new seaside paradise gets around.

The sea is one natural resource that Texas has never exploited fully in the past. Now that places like Palm Beach and Cap d'Antibes are getting crowded, Texans are hastening to remedy that omission.

12: Father Ballí's Island

Iowe, Jr.

Padre Island surf, from a jetty

PEOPLE who have never viewed the Gulf of Mexico from any point except the sheltered Florida coast, where it is normally as gentle as a pond, have missed a close acquaintance with one of the world's great seas. The 600,000 square miles encompassed in the Gulf are exceeded only by the Malay Sea, the Caribbean next door to it, the Mediterranean, and the Bering Sea.

Of all these less-than-ocean-wide bodies of water, only the Caribbean is generally deeper. Indeed, the Gulf and the Caribbean are so intimately connected that they might well be considered a single maritime highway—a Central American Sea.

As everybody who has traveled the Gulf extensively in anything from a shrimp boat to an ocean liner can testify, it is nothing like the tranquil lake that it appears to be from the placid shores of Sarasota, Clearwater, or Pensacola.

From early June to late September, some of the most riotous hurricanes ever seen are likely to run amok in the Gulf. Almost invariably they head for the 600 miles of coast between Brownsville and New Orleans. At any season squalls blow up, riding on white-crested waves that whirl and meet like polo ponies.

Beaches that look to the east, in the direction from which the prevailing winds blow, usually have the most boisterous surf. The Gulf is no exception. From Veracruz to Galveston and beyond, a visitor with a taste for exploration finds a succession of broad, level beaches, facing endless ranks of breakers that drift in, foaming, as if from the vast reaches of the Atlantic. All but a few of these beaches, in the vicinity of coastal cities, are utterly deserted.

Until a few years ago, the loneliest strand on all this length of nearly empty shore was the match-thin strip called Padre Island, paralleling the South Texas mainland between Brownsville and Corpus Christi. Unbroken for 131 miles from Port Isabel to Port Aransas, it was—and is—the longest stretch of hard-sand beach anywhere in the civilized world. With a sturdy car and a full tank of gasoline, you can drive from one end to the other.

Before the last link of the Intracoastal Canal was extended to Brownsville, through the shallow lagoon that forms the back side of Padre Island, it would have been hard to find a more desolate place for a vacation trip than this curving line of sand, bordered by dunes and brush.

Gold

Oil rig on the South Texas coast

Padre Island sand dunes

Nautical charts showed only two noteworthy features in its entire length. One was an abandoned oil drum, half buried on the shore. The other was a spar in the water that was supposed to mark the site of a submerged wreck—and the spar had disappeared. The island's only inhabitants were sea gulls, wild ducks and geese, and an occasional half-wild steer that wandered over from the mainland.

Today, a motorist who finds himself stranded on the beach has only to walk a mile or so to the other side. There he will come within hail of a stream of barges, fishing boats, and pleasure craft, passing by on the inland waterway. The island still is lonely and deserted. But it has become the margin of a busy marine highway.

Padre Island got its name from a sea-going Spanish priest, Father Nicolás Ballí, who once owned it. Back in 1804, when Spain ruled all of Mexico including Texas, King Charles IV granted the island to Padre Nicolás—along with a portion of the Rio Grande Valley—for a mission and cattle ranch. The good father founded the Rancho de la Santa Cruz, fifteen miles up the coast from present-day Port Isabel. After his death, it was carried on by his nephews and nieces.

Several other colonies later settled on the island, during the years when Texas enjoyed a thriving coastal trade in merchant schooners. One was established by Captain John V. Singer—brother of Isaac Singer, who patented the first sewing machine—after his ship went aground in 1847.

With his crew member and companion, Joanna Shaw, Singer made his home twenty-five miles up the beach from the heirs of Father Ballí.

The coastal trade languished after Texas divorced Mexico, and disappeared entirely during the Civil War. Captain Singer and his friend departed. The other colonists—including Father Ballí's heirs—died or drifted away. Their homes and corrals were scattered by storms, washed by tides breaking through into the lagoon, and buried by winds that blew across the shifting dunes. In a few years, nothing remained to show that the Padre's Island had ever been inhabited.

Over on the mainland, though, some changes of a more permanent kind were made. They were the work of a pair of Irish traders, Captain Richard King and Captain Mifflin Kenedy, who like Singer had carried freight along the coast.

In 1852, King acquired 54,000 acres of grassland on Santa Gertrudis Creek, which flows into an arm of the Laguna Madre near the present city of Kingsville, below Corpus Christi. A few years later, Kenedy joined him in the cattle business.

During the Civil War they sold beef and horses to the Confederate Army, while their ships ran cotton through the Union blockade. With the profits they acquired more land. By 1868, when they dissolved the partnership and split their holdings, they owned nearly all the coast for seventy miles along the lagoon, in what are now Kenedy and Kleberg Counties.

Kenedy's La Parra Ranch, covering about 375 square miles, was eventually sold to a Kansas City syndicate. King's original Santa Ger-

High water in Kenedy County

Quincy Howe, Jr.

Quincy Howe, Jr.

Children wade in a creek at Kingsville

trudis Ranch grew into the great King Ranch, in four separate parcels adding up to 1,525 square miles—an area considerably larger than Rhode Island. It is owned and operated by his descendants.

The legends hovering over this feudal domain are reminiscent of *The Arabian Nights,* and have been told as many times. The facts have been told too, most recently in a book by Tom Lea, the novelist and painter who lives in El Paso. In essence, the facts are that while Richard King built an enormous cattle dominion, modeled on an old-time Spanish hacienda, the progeny of Robert Justus Kleberg, who married his daughter, have managed it as a modern corporation.

The ranch hands are secretive Mexican *vaqueros,* some of whom have never stepped off its land. All the activities on the ranch are conducted in Spanish. But the methods used in breeding stock and grazing them are the most advanced techniques of biological science.

The King Ranch first imported high-grade English cattle from Kentucky, to improve the wild native Longhorns. Later on they developed their own Santa Gertrudis strain, the only recognized variety of purebred cattle originating in America. Years ago they planted tough Rhodes grass from Africa. Since then they have perfected a special type of yellow-beard grass. Various other innovations have come from the King Ranch.

The huge white mansion at the Santa Gertrudis Ranch headquarters, near Kingsville, with twenty-five rooms, a ten-car garage, and a swimming pool, is used for entertainment and to house distinguished guests. But Robert Justus Kleberg Jr., president of this cattle company, lives nearby in a modest seven-room ranch house. The Klebergs are lordly, and rule their immense preserve according to their own ideas. But so, probably, does the chief executive of any large family-owned enterprise.

There was a time when it wasn't possible to drive straight from Brownsville to Corpus Christi. The highway went a few miles out of Raymondville into Kenedy County, and ended where it met the southernmost segment of the King Ranch.

Today a fine paved turnpike runs all the way to Bishop, by and through parts of the King dominions, and on into Corpus Christi. A connecting link even cuts across the Santa Gertrudis Ranch from Kingsville, in the direction of Duval County.

The fifty-six miles from Raymondville to Riviera, at the southeast corner of the Santa Gertrudis, are only a trifle less lonely than the length of Padre Island, which they parallel. Next to Loving and King Counties in West Texas, Kenedy is the state's least populous, with 884 people.

218   The roadside settlements known as Rudolph, Armstrong, Mifflin, and Sarita are little more than freight stations for cattle on the railroad that accompanies the highway. In addition, Sarita has a county courthouse.

Not an ounce of gasoline is for sale in any of these inhabited places. For that matter, nothing else is for sale either. There are no commercial establishments of any kind in Kenedy County. It has no bank deposits, because there aren't any banks.

By contrast, Kleberg County is almost a cosmopolitan watering place. The King Ranch occupies about three-fourths of it, in two divisions that meet at the crossing of San Fernando Creek, on the Nueces County line to the north. Between the Santa Gertrudis and the Laureles divisions lies a rich farming district, watered by little streams that empty into the maze of bayous and lagoons known collectively as Baffin Bay. The capital of this agricultural island in a sea of grass is the small city of Kingsville.

Originally, Kingsville was a hamlet on the railroad, like Sarita or Mifflin, where trains stopped for visitors to the ranch. It was also the county seat, and had a courthouse where births and deaths and marriages could be recorded. Then it began to grow, as the business carried on at the ranch became bigger and more complex, and farmers moved in to grow cotton and food crops.

In 1925, Kingsville acquired a state educational institution, the Texas College of Arts and Industries. In World War II the town was

Quincy Howe, Jr.

Saddlemaker in Kingsville

Hotel Robert Driscoll (right) overlooks the White Plaza in Corpus Christi

chosen as the site of a large U.S. Naval Auxiliary Air Station teaching young officers to fly. Today Kingsville has more than 25,000 citizens, and has achieved a measure of freedom from its former status as a King Ranch colony.

Another influence which has contributed to Kingsville's increasing independence is the oil industry. Since 1940 Kleberg County has become an important oil-producing area, and it is just across the line from Nueces County, the leader in South Texas. Most of the wells are on land that belongs to the King Ranch, though a good many are in the Laguna Madre, which belongs to the state. But the engineers, geologists, and roughnecks

220   belong to neither the King Ranch nor the state. In Kleberg County they generally work for the Humble Oil & Refining Company—a Standard Oil subsidiary—and Kingsville is their capital too.

Oil has brought the usual industrial development to the countryside. Just beyond the county line, at Bishop, is an enormous chemical plant owned by the Celanese Corporation of America. Smaller plants around it handle petroleum products and recycle gas from wells in South Texas. The longest pipe line in the nation passes by here, carrying natural gas from the Valley to New York City. The King Ranch loads cattle for shipment from its pens at Bishop.

A few miles east of Bishop is another great ranch of a different kind. Probably the only cotton farm in the country large enough to justify its name is the Chapman Ranch, on Agua Dulce Creek, which flows from Nueces County into a branch of Baffin Bay. It covers about fifty-five square miles, of which thirty-three are under cultivation.

Its reticent owner, John Chapman, applies the same scientific methods to agriculture that have done so well for the Klebergs in the cattle business. At one time Chapman was said to pay the highest personal income tax in Nueces County.

That may not be true any longer, even though Chapman's enterprises are as sound as ever. For the coastal region surrounding Corpus Christi Bay has prospered mightily in the last few years. As late as 1950, though it had the solid beginnings of an industrial economy, Corpus Christi still was a rather large and sunny resort city, with a handsome waterfront, devoted mainly to fishing and pleasure. The vast oil and chemical complex, reaching down the Gulf shore from Houston and its environs, so far had only lapped at Corpus Christi's door.

The port of Corpus Christi

Quincy Howe, Jr.

Howe, Jr.

Corpus Christi Cathedral

The reasons were various. One was that Corpus Christi's port facilities were insufficient for a large volume of ocean trade. Though it has one of the finest natural harbors on the coast, the channels were tricky and the docks inadequate. Another reason, much less obvious at first glance, was that Corpus Christi lacked the flow of fresh water needed for most large industrial operations.

It may seem odd that a city surrounded by bays and inlets, as Corpus Christi is, at the end of a river winding down off the Edwards Plateau in West Texas, would lack a plentiful supply of water. But the southern coast of Texas, though it faces a tropical sea, is a semi-arid land. Corpus Christi, for example, receives only twenty-eight inches of rain in a year, compared with the forty-eight inches that fall at Galveston, and even more at Beaumont, near the lush bayous of Louisiana. The lower Gulf Coast is something like the shore line of North Africa, where shining white cities look out over the Mediterranean from the margin of the desert.

Fortunately South Texas isn't as dry as the Sahara. But it has to guard its water, and look for new sources when it wants to build up either its agriculture or its industry. Basically, it is a grassland, differing from West Texas only in that its background is the sea instead of the mountains.

Corpus Christi solved its water problem—for the next few years, at least—by throwing a dam across the Nueces River near the town of Mathis, thirty-five miles away. Completed in 1958, Wesley Seale Dam backs up enough water to support ten times the productive activity that goes on around the city today.

The harbor problem has been solved too—by deepening the channel, widening the entrance to the port, and building tons of modern cargo-handling equipment. The new Harbor Bridge, opened up in 1959 above the mouth of the dockside area, is high enough to carry traffic over the mastheads of the tallest ships afloat.

Without question, Corpus Christi has the most beautiful harbor on the coast. The city looks out over a series of shallow basins, lined with tiers of steps like an amphitheater opening off the bay. They are reserved for the picturesque hulls of yachts and fishing boats, while utilitarian vessels are routed into a narrow arm of the deep-water channel, hidden away on the other side of town. Landscaped parks and driveways extend out on the quays where yachts tie up.

The skyline of Corpus Christi is dominated by a strip of esplanade on a terrace above the downtown business district. Here stand the cathedral and—side by side—the two largest hotels, the White Plaza and the Robert Driscoll. The hotels remain as a dual monument to one of the most rousing feuds that ever rocked Corpus Christi.

Father Balli's Island

Among the financiers of the White Plaza, in the booming 1920's, was the late Colonel Robert Driscoll, son of an old-time cattleman who had made a fortune in beef and oil. When the colonel died in 1929, he left his sister Clara as the sole proprietor of their joint inheritance.

Clara Driscoll was *mucha mujer,* even by Texas standards. A fiery redhead, she could ride, fight, drink, and swear with the gusto of a cow-puncher. By the time she was twenty-five, she had written two published novels and a musical comedy called *Mexicana,* produced on Broadway by the Shuberts. Later on she was a Democratic National Committee-woman and backer of John Nance Garner for President.

New Harbor Bridge in Corpus Christi

Iowe, Jr.

Quincy Howe, Jr.

A home on the Corpus Christi waterfront

The operator of the White Plaza (then simply the Plaza) was a silver-throated ex-vaudeville singer named Jack White, who later served as mayor of San Antonio. During the depression—while Clara was in Chile as the wife of Ambassador Hal Sevier, founder of the Austin *American*—White gained control of the hotel, along with two others in San Antonio and Dallas. On her return, Clara tried to wrest it from him by foreclosure. A Federal court heard the case, and ruled against her.

Clara had never had any use for Jack White anyway. She swore a mighty oath that she would build a hotel next to the White Plaza, so tall that she could stand at a window and vent her displeasure on it in the most suitable way that occurred to her. And so she did.

The lavish Hotel Robert Driscoll cost her $3,500,000, and went up four stories higher than the White Plaza. Clara lived on the top floor—in an enormous penthouse with twelve bathrooms—until her death in 1945. Part of that penthouse now is reserved for the Klebergs when they come to town.

Such was the esteem in which Texans held Clara Driscoll, when she died, that her body was taken to San Antonio and allowed to lie in

Quincy Howe, Jr.

Church of the Good Shepherd, Corpus Christi

state in the Alamo, which her money and influence had helped to preserve.

With Port Aransas, the fishing village and resort town at the entrance to the bay, Corpus Christi now ranks third among the harbor systems of Texas, and eighth in the nation—behind San Francisco and ahead of Los Angeles. Its total tonnage in 1949 was about twenty-four million, of which Port Aransas contributed almost six million. The biggest outgoing shipments are of crude oil. The main import is aluminum ore, for the big Reynolds plant at Ingleside, across the bay.

Corpus Christi has acres of oil refineries, chemical plants converting oyster shells into various ingredients for industry, and a big zinc smelter using ore shipped in by sea from other places. Among its more exotic businesses are onion seeds and food products—starch, dextrose, fodder for animals—made from milo maize, a new variety of corn introduced along the coast during World War II. The Naval Air Station at the south end of the bay is the largest in America.

In spite of all these useful and remunerative activities—which can be expected to grow in the years ahead—Corpus Christi's heart is in the amiable occupation of entertaining visitors. Since the 1920's, when Colonel

Driscoll began to build the White Plaza, Corpus Christi has been haunted by the dream of turning the barren length of Padre Island into a great coastal playground—a South Texas Riviera.

For almost half a century, after the early settlers wandered off, the only permanent resident on the island was an Irishman named Pat Dunn, who used it for a cattle ranch. He lived across the Laguna Madre from Corpus Christi, in a mansion built out of rare specimens of driftwood which he picked up on the beach, until a hurricane came along in 1916 and blew it all away. Then he put up a modest ranch home which is still there.

Ten years after the hurricane a real-estate promoter, Colonel Sam Robertson, turned up with the idea of developing the island into a resort, and bought most of Dunn's land. He built the Surfside Hotel and half a dozen cottages on the beach, and stretched a three-mile trestle over the lagoon, with wooden troughs to guide the wheels of motorists. Another hurricane swept over the island in 1933, and blew Colonel Robertson's resort away.

After that the beach lay dormant again until 1950. Then Nueces County laid a solid causeway four miles long and 300 feet wide across the lagoon, bearing a concrete highway. Three tracts of land were set aside for parks. A pier for fishermen was built out into the Gulf. Restaurants, motor courts, and shops went up.

A toll road now runs northward fifteen miles through the dunes to Port Aransas, at the other end of Mustang Island. (A patch of water once separated Mustang from the rest of Padre Island. Though it has long since disappeared, folks around the bay still think of them as two islands.) Beach homes—some of them spacious and expensive—have begun to rise along this Côte d'Azur.

Padre Island has a long way to go yet, before it blossoms into a palm-lined vista of hotels, mansions, and casinos, all the way from Port Isabel to Port Aransas. For one thing, it needs a highway down the rest of this waste of sand.

For another, it needs more towns along the mainland—especially in the solitude of Kenedy County—if only so that the islanders can flee to them when hurricanes come howling in toward the coast. From the middle of Padre Island to either end is a mighty long ride in a tropical torrent of wind and water.

But there is plenty of time. The beach was there long before Father Ballí found it. No doubt it will be there still when Texans are ready for an island paradise all their own.

13: Costa Rica

A tanker passes through residential Port Arthur

*I*T all began on the rim of an ancient salt mound, a few miles out of Beaumont, when the new century was eleven days old. Before that, from the Rio Grande to the Sabine, the coast lay drowsing in the sun. Cattle grazed on the prairie, beside rivers that drifted through silent meadows to the sea. In the countryside beyond the meadows, children wearing faded overalls bent down among the dusty rows of cotton. Crows called from the pecan groves along the rivers. Buzzards wheeled in the high white sierras overhead.

An engineer from Austria, who had once been a naval officer, changed all that. His name was Anthony Lucas, and he worked as a technical consultant in the sulphur mines of Louisiana. Captain Lucas had an idea that if you dug down under the salt domes where sulphur was found, you might discover oil. He had searched for it in Louisiana, without any luck.

One day toward the end of the old era, Lucas met a prospector named Patillo Higgins, from Beaumont. Higgins also thought that a salt dome was a likely place to look for oil, and he too had sunk a well without success. Higgins had a lease on 1,000 acres of land just south of Beaumont.

The two men pooled their resources, and started drilling under a mound on the Higgins lease. On January 11, 1901, when the drill was down 1,160 feet, the well blew in. A column of oil and gas thundered up out of the ground, bringing the drill and the casing with it, and sprayed petroleum around the countryside for nine days before they were able to get it capped.

Theirs was the world's first gusher, and its name was Spindletop. It produced half as much oil in a day as all the other wells in the United States put together. And it changed the face of Texas forever. With Spindletop, the old empire of cattle and cotton began to fade in Texas, and a modern industrial democracy began to evolve.

Though many imposing structures have been raised upon it through the years that followed Spindletop, the basic industry of Texas still is oil. If the Texas-owned companies on the New York Stock Exchange can be considered representative, at least half are in the business of producing, refining, or distributing petroleum and its by-products—or else of rendering essential services to that business. Even the glamorous workshops that design electronic gadgets got their start making instruments for oil exploration.

Drilling a gas well in a Port Arthur suburb

230   The vast chemical complex, which has spread over the Gulf Coast since World War II, is largely an outgrowth of the esoteric art of dividing petroleum into its various constituents, and then combining them into other things. The steel industry in Texas fabricates material for well casings, pipe lines, and storage tanks. Shipyards in Beaumont, Port Arthur, and Galveston build tankers and barges and supply vessels for offshore drilling platforms.

The economic climate in Texas depends mainly on the weather in the oil business. For some time now, the atmosphere has been heavy. Oil has poured abundantly from wells and refineries, while the public thirst for it has been moderate. Supplies of oil and gasoline have accumulated on storage farms, while prices have been going down.

The oil industry faces a peculiar dilemma. The pools from which it draws the volatile fluid are by no means inexhaustible. In time, they 'run dry. If the fountain is to keep flowing, exploration must go on, turning up new fields to replace the old ones. But exploration is costly, and often

Tanker tying up at a dock

Quincy

A roughneck mixes mud to lubricate a drill bit

disappointing. When a rich producer finally comes in, the temptation to let it cascade from the ground is almost irresistible.

So the oil industry—and the Railroad Commission that regulates it in Texas—try to maintain a delicate balance between starvation and surfeit. With one hand they encourage the prospector to go on searching for new reserves. With the other they do their best to restrain him from drinking too heartily at the spring, when he stumbles onto it out of the desert.

That dilemma accounts for much of the flamboyance in Texas finance, which often perplexes people from other places. They assume that industry is simply a matter of finding some essential commodity, and then producing enough of it to meet the demand. But oil doesn't work that way. It swings erratically between impoverishment and plenty. And so does the mood of Texas industry with it.

By far the greatest concentration of heavy industry in Texas—and the kernel from which the rest has grown—is clustered around two port systems about seventy-five miles apart. One is the group of cities close to Sabine Lake, at the border of Louisiana. The other is the larger assemblage on Galveston Bay. The country between them is relatively untouched, except by fleeting glimpses of the mammoth trucks that race along the highway, bearing lengths of pipe, portable derricks, and drilling equipment.

Sabine Lake is formed by the Sabine River, flowing down through the forests of East Texas, and is fed by the Neches River, a few miles to the west. The cities around it have names and separate identities. There is Beaumont—the largest—on the Neches, near the site of Spindletop. Orange is on the Sabine, where Louisiana begins. Port Arthur looks out on the lake.

Together they form a triangle pointing toward the Gulf. Between them are lesser communities: Nederland, Port Neches, Groves. But they are really all one entity—shopping districts placed at intervals in the midst of a huge industrial center.

The chemical plants and refineries stretch for miles along all the navigable channels. Their names read like a roster of the petroleum industry and the specialties associated with it. Texaco has an enormous refinery at Port Arthur and an asphalt plant at Port Neches. Atlantic Refining, Gulf Oil, Magnolia Petroleum, Pure Oil, and Sun Oil are scattered over the landscape nearby.

Du Pont produces nylon salt outside of Orange, and has another plant near Port Neches. Allied Chemical, American Cyanamid, Koppers, and Olin Mathieson produce ethylenes, polyethylenes, and other petro-chemicals. Goodrich and United States Rubber both convert butadiene into synthetic rubber at Port Neches, and Goodyear is building a plant near Beaumont.

Jones & Laughlin and United States Steel fabricate metal containers for gas and oil at Port Arthur. Standard Brass makes valves and fittings. These are some of the great national corporations. Then there are smaller firms of local importance, like Ellerbee Brothers (steel fabricators), Neches Butane, Port Iron, and Sabine Steel. The Burton Company and the Gulfport Corporation, in Port Arthur, and Levingston, at Orange, build tugs, boats, and barges and provide dry-dock facilities for ships.

Brown & Root, Incorporated

A derrick assembles an offshore drilling platform

Sabine Lake is a port system second only to Galveston Bay in Texas, and ranks as the sixth in the nation, after New Orleans and Baton Rouge. Beaumont handled more than half its fifty million total tons in 1959. As in the case of most other Texas ports, the principal cargoes are crude oil and petroleum products.

A considerable fraction of Sabine Lake's maritime trade—though it wouldn't be likely to show up in tonnage figures—is of a kind that occasionally makes even fresh-water sailors smile. It is the work of building, operating, and servicing the massive offshore platforms from which prospectors drill for oil in the Gulf.

Between Galveston and the bayous of Louisiana—where the coastal shelf is wide and comparatively shallow—these artificial islands loom on piers above the water, as if they had been marooned on the peaks of a submerged continent.

The crews live aboard them in comfortable quarters, making the run ashore at intervals in company boats. Garbage disposal is a simple problem—the cooks heave it over the side. The refuse brings fish, and the men catch them for dinner, completing what biologists refer to as a "closed ecological cycle." Weekend parties in luxurious cabin cruisers often congregate around the platforms, where the fish are.

When these nautical wells need to be serviced, sea-going technicians in trucks filled with electronic gear ride out on barges, and log the contours of the earth strata down below the Gulf. If the well is a good one, its flow is piped into the holds of transfer barges, and towed in to a tank farm or a refinery on shore.

Until May 31, 1960, drilling was rather desultory in the Texas end of the Gulf. The state was wary of granting leases more than three miles off the coast, until its title all the way out to the historic 10½-mile limit was assured. Then the Supreme Court handed down a decision reaffirming the fact that Texas owns its tidelands. Since then, offshore activity has been getting brisk.

On land, in a new field of exploration, a wildcatter expects to drill about nine dry holes before he brings in a good well. That's why the Internal Revenue Service allows a special tax deduction, called depletion, on income from oil and gas. Without this allowance, the risk of failure might become prohibitive, and the nation would suffer from a fuel shortage.

In the Gulf, the odds are better. About one shaft in three turns out to be a producer. A good many marine wells produce gas, which finds a readier market nowadays than oil. Even though it costs more to sink a well from a platform raised on stilts above the water, the risk is less than it is ashore. So the Texas petroleum industry is gradually moving out to sea.

As time goes on and new ways of getting at the sunken treasure are devised, the Gulf Coast could become a floating forest of derricks from Galveston to New Orleans. At its widest point, south of Lake Charles, Louisiana, the edge of the coastal shelf lies more than 100 miles from the mainland. From the shallow bed of the sea could conceivably arise an offshore Venice of refineries and chemical plants, docks and living quarters, to process the submarine flow at its source, replacing the present laborious task of towing it in to the nearest port. Fantastic as the idea may seem, the Soviet Union has just such a city on stilts in the Caspian Sea, sixty miles out from the port of Baku.

But that's a project for the future. Today, each of the few hundred offshore platforms is as lonely as a lighthouse on an uninhabited reef. In most cases they are beyond sight of land or of any other object except an occasional passing ship.

Oil of a different kind comes from the water in this part of the Gulf. Fishing boats from Sabine Lake and Galveston Bay net enormous quantities of menhaden. They are not intended for anybody's dinner table. Instead they are ground up into oil and fertilizer in factories by the docks. Almost half of all the marine life caught by commercial fishermen from Texas ports is menhaden.

Texans are not particularly fond of seafood anyway, even on the coast. Steak is their native dish—and cattle can be found anywhere in Texas, even on the seashore.

More than 90 per cent of all the edible fish brought in by the commercial fleet are shrimp—and most of them are packed for shipment to other parts. The rest—consisting mainly of red snapper, drum, oysters, trout, and redfish—satisfy the occasional whim of Texas diners for something out of the sea.

One of the finest seafood restaurants anywhere in Texas used to be Granger's, a collection of small dining rooms in an unpretentious frame building on the shore at Sabine Pass, where the ship channels from Orange, Beaumont, and Port Arthur issue jointly into the Gulf.

Boasting that it caught its own fish daily from a squadron that tied up at its back door, Granger's catered mostly to hunting and fishing parties from other states. In 1959 the restaurant caught fire and burned to the ground. It has not been rebuilt.

A few miles out of Beaumont, on the mainland, you would hardly

**Governor Daniel's brother Bill—now Governor of Guam—
in a civic celebration with Vera, his wife**

Galveston bathers congregate by the Balinese Room pier

know that all this maritime trade and industry exist. The countryside is drowsy under ragged shawls of Spanish moss. Its towns—Anahuac, Dayton, Liberty—are rural shopping centers. (Liberty is best known to the world outside of Texas as the home of Governor Price Daniel's personable brother Bill, a lawyer, sometime actor with John Wayne in *The Alamo,* and a governor in his own right, by presidential appointment to the Island of Guam.)

Around these market towns, the outstanding source of income is rice. Texas has about half a million soggy acres planted in rice, reaching out along the coast for 100 miles on either side of Houston. It alternates with Louisiana as the No. 1 producer.

The world's largest rice mill is the Comet plant at Beaumont. Comet also has mills in Houston and Bay City (down the coast a way, toward Corpus Christi), in New Orleans, and in Stuttgart, Arkansas. Its buff-colored packages are found on grocery shelves everywhere.

From Sabine Pass, a highway runs along the shore to Port Bolivar, at the entrance to Galveston Bay. For thirty miles or so, almost into the town of High Island (which is not an island) near the head of Bolivar Peninsula, the beach is as bare as most of Padre Island. The entire length of sand and surf belongs to a Beaumont lawyer, Caldwell McFaddin, and his family, one of the old cattle clans of East Texas. They don't object to people using it, but the waterfront is not for sale. They like it as it is.

Costa Rica

Costa Rica

Costa Rica

At High Island, a new freeway from Houston comes down to the shore, after circling around Galveston Bay. From there to Port Bolivar, the Peninsula has developed into a middle-income sea resort for the populace of Houston.

Some 3,000 beach houses have gone up on this knife-thin neck of land in the last few years. The majority are cottages perched on stilts above the sand—in case of high water—but a number are substantial summer homes. For week-end visitors, there are motels with kitchenettes. The State Highway Department operates a free ferry between Port Bolivar and Galveston.

A century ago any reasonable person would have told you without hesitation that Galveston was destined to become the great city of Texas. Already it was the largest, and the only one founded on a busy ocean commerce.

Galveston had certain deceptive resemblances to New York City. For one, it was on an island. For another, it boasted an advantage that no other Texas city then enjoyed—a fine natural harbor, capable of sheltering a good part of the world's shipping at one time. Besides that, Galveston people were cosmopolitan, energetic, and convinced of their future eminence. Galveston had the look of a city headed for the financial importance that Manhattan had achieved already.

But Dallas, and then San Antonio, and then Houston overtook Galveston. While it kept growing—except for one benumbed decade between 1900 and 1910—it never quite caught up with the breath-taking progress of Texas as a whole. One city after another passed it by. Today Galveston is far back in fifteenth place among the cities of Texas, behind such upstart leaders as Corpus Christi, Beaumont, Wichita Falls, and Odessa.

The reason usually cited is the stunning effect of the hurricane. Everybody knows how that furious windstorm roared in from the Gulf at noon on September 8, 1900, swamped the whole of Galveston Island under a couple of fathoms of crashing surf, wrecked nearly all of the city's wealth, and receded in the early morning of the next day, leaving up to 8,000 people dead and 500 more of them so dazed that they never regained their reason. The Galveston hurricane was the most crushing civic disaster in American history, outdoing the human damage done by either the Chicago fire or the San Francisco earthquake.

Yet the city recovered. Its $30,000,000 in lost property was rebuilt, this time of more durable materials. A concrete sea wall ten miles long and seventeen feet high was raised along the beach. The port was

240   dredged and deepened, and provided with acres of docks, warehouses, grain elevators, rail spurs, and modern handling facilities. Two wide causeways were laid across the channel to the mainland. With all of these improvements, Galveston remains a leisurely little coast city of fewer than 70,000 inhabitants.

The explanation probably lies in a fact of nature more fundamental than the hurricane. Unlike Manhattan Island, Galveston is not situated on the margin of a continent, where the sea ends and the land begins. The bay reaches inland for twenty-seven miles beyond Galveston. The land continues on for almost 1,000 miles in the other direction.

The first railroad across Texas bypassed the coast, with its inlets, bays, and bayous, and took the easier route through Houston. When Houston dug a ship channel down Buffalo Bayou to the bay, it saved consigners of cargo about forty miles of relatively expensive transportation by rail, and gave them another forty miles of relatively cheap transportation by water.

Besides, Galveston has been slow to make full use of its own situation. The island is only about two miles wide, though it stretches for

A battered survivor of the Galveston hurricane

Quincy Howe,

A cargo ship loads flour at a Galveston dock

twenty miles more down the coast, beyond the city. There isn't room, close in to the port, for expansive industries like the ones that line the Houston ship channel.

But right across the harbor, facing the docks, is a level tract of undeveloped land that belongs to Galveston. Known as Pelican Island, it contains more than six square miles of almost empty real estate. Only in the last few years has Galveston bestirred itself to improve this neighboring area for industry.

If Galveston were a business enterprise, you might say that its management for the past century has been in the hands of one family, the Moodys. William L. Moody, Sr., went to Galveston as a young man before the Civil War, opened a law office, and built up a cotton brokerage firm on the side.

His son, the late W. L. Moody, Jr., branched out into banking, insurance, hotels, and a host of other profitable activities. When he died in 1954, Moody was reputed to be among the ten richest men in the United States. His holdings reached far beyond the confines of Galveston.

The Moody-owned American National Life Insurance Company is one of the twenty largest in the nation, with policies worth at least 2½ billion dollars. Their Affiliated National Hotels include hostelries in Washington, D.C., Indianapolis, Omaha, Norfolk, Birmingham, Mobile, and New Orleans, in addition to Dallas and eight other Texas cities, and the Buccaneer, the Galvez, the Jean Lafitte, and two others in Galveston.

The Moodys publish both Galveston newspapers, the morning *News* and the afternoon *Tribune*. There is literally almost nothing in the city of a profitable nature that they aren't interested in.

Under the influence of the Moodys, Galveston has leaned toward commerce and entertainment rather than basic industry. There are few productive activities of any size in Galveston. Among those few are the Todd Shipyards on Pelican Island.

Notably abstemious in their personal habits, the Moodys let Galveston make a name for itself as a town devoted to the pursuit of pleasure. Under the benign eye of the late Sam Maceo, polite drinking, dining, and gambling flourished openly in the luxurious Balinese Room, on a private pier out over the beach. They could also be found in a variety of less elegant places around the city.

Since Maceo's death, all but the more discreet forms of amusement have been banished. Much of the gambling has moved into new quarters at resorts down the coast.

Despite its rather Old World atmosphere, and its appearance of

Howe, Jr.

A chemical plant at Texas City

244   being inhabited solely by guests at its hotels and motor courts, Galveston is an important port. It loads more sulphur than any other maritime city, and leads the United States in shipments of grain. It ranks among the leaders in exports of cotton and cattle, and in imports of sugar and fruit.

The difference between Galveston and Corpus Christi or Port Arthur is that its cargoes—like the people sunning themselves on its beach—simply pass through Galveston. They come from other places, and are going somewhere else.

From its fine harbor, Galveston can look across the bay and see the vapor drifting from the chemical plants, the smelter, the fertilizer factories, and the refineries at Texas City, on the mainland.

Texas City is less than half the size of Galveston. Its port handles practically nothing except its own products. Yet they amount to more than twice the tonnage passing through Galveston.

Maybe the opening up of Pelican Island will change all that, and Galveston will emerge from the nineteenth century at last.

14: Houston, the Metropolis

**Farmer plows while a supermarket
goes up around him in Houston**

*I*N some ways, Houston is a paradoxical city. For example, it is one of the busiest ports in the nation, running neck-and-neck with New Orleans for second place, after New York City. Yet it shows no visible evidence of its maritime importance. No broad river runs beside it, with docks and cargo sheds and glimpses of tall masts between the buildings on its downtown streets. The Ship Channel is a devious trail of water winding over the prairie, from a point about five miles east of the business district.

Again, while metropolitan Houston has perhaps a million and a quarter people, and the monuments and institutions that go with them, it gives the impression of being an overgrown country town, occupied with nothing of greater consequence than selling a little real estate and insurance. As in Lubbock or Amarillo, blocks of towering skyscrapers stand next to acres of parking lots, surrounded by shops a story or two tall.

Though it serves the vast expanse of plains and mountains to the west, Houston has more of the easygoing character associated with the South. It would not seem out of place in Alabama or Mississippi. Within sight of its steel-and-concrete towers, Harris County grazes more beef cattle than any other similar area in the country. In its suburbs, stubborn farmers have been known to keep on plowing while supermarkets went up around them.

In fact, it is hard to fix or define the atmosphere of Houston. Possibly because of its size and the conglomerate nature of its interests, it conforms less to any recognizeable pattern than other Texas cities. Houston is a teeming and peculiar kind of organism all to itself. The one genetic trait which it shares unquestionably with the rest of Texas is a talent for doing anything it does at all in a big way.

Houston came into existence as a real-estate speculation, four months after the victory of Sam Houston over Mexican General Santa Anna on the nearby bank of the San Jacinto River. Its founders were a pair of spellbinding promoters from New York, the brothers Augustus and John K. Allen.

Immigrants were swarming into the Texas Republic, some across the Sabine River from Louisiana and some through the port of Galveston. It struck the Allens as a good idea to build a town where the two routes met, at the farthest navigable point on the crooked stream called Buffalo Bayou.

246

Bayou east of Houston

Quincy

They opened up for business on August 30, 1836, selling lots at $1 an acre. Before long they had 500 fellow citizens—most of them, like the Allens, engaged in land speculation. For three years, the government of Texas was persuaded to make Houston its capital. After that the city grew by sheer determination, coupled with judicious aid from friends in high places.

As an instance, there was the first railroad in Texas. The Buffalo Bayou, Brazos & Colorado—now a part of the Southern Pacific—was chartered by the State Legislature in 1850. It started in Houston, and eventually got as far as San Antonio. The second railroad went from Galveston to Houston, where it met the first one. They gave Houston a running start as a transportation center—a lead which it has never lost.

Houston's rail connections came in handy at the turn of the century, when a boundless supply of oil was found at Spindletop, only seventy-five miles away. As the nearest commercial capital to Beaumont—and by that time the second city of Texas, creeping up on San Antonio—Houston got in on the ground floor of the oil boom. It became the principal market and source of equipment for the new petroleum industry. Soon after, the great field at Humble turned up on the outskirts of Houston, followed by another one at Goose Creek. From then on, Houston's commanding position in the oil business was assured.

Meanwhile, another of Houston's good friends had been at work. He was Brigadier General Henry M. Robert, division chief of the U. S. Army Engineers in the Gulf area—and the author of the parliamentary bible, Robert's *Rules of Order*.

In 1897, Robert had recommended to the Congress of the United States that $2,500,000 be appropriated to provide a modern ship channel down the tortuous twenty-five-mile length of Buffalo Bayou to the bay. After the usual delays, half the money was authorized, if Houston would put up the other half. Houston bestirred itself, and did.

The Ship Channel was completed in 1914. From that year, the rise of Houston to its present eminence can be dated. In his book, *Houston: Land of the Big Rich,* Houston's own George Fuermann points out with disarming candor that tonnage figures for an oil port can be deceptive—that liquid petroleum, flowing into the holds of tankers at Houston's docks, brings in far less revenue to the port than the dry cargoes heaved aboard freighters by the stevedores at Galveston.

Of course that's true—but Houston wasn't after the fees for handling its merchandise. The Ship Channel gave Houston direct access by sea to the world's markets for gasoline and other oil products. Refineries moved

Buffalo Speedway approaching the city

in along the banks, converting the crude oil that gushed from the wells around Houston.

Ever since, Houston has been looked on as an ideal site for heavy industry in Texas. The other profitable and creative enterprises which have accrued to it with the years—steel fabrication, chemicals, drilling tools, construction companies, pipe lines, and all the rest—have come to Houston on the strength of its canny resolve to invent the one resource it lacked, which was a harbor.

With these assets working for it, by 1930 Houston had pulled ahead of both Dallas and San Antonio, to become the foremost city of Texas. But the truly big growth that was to make Houston the seventh city of the nation—just back of Baltimore and in front of Cleveland—still lay ahead. It began toward the close of the 1930's, while Jesse Jones of Houston was

head of the Reconstruction Finance Corporation—the New Deal agency
that lent money to ailing industries—and continued after Jones became
Franklin D. Roosevelt's wartime Secretary of Commerce.

Jesse Jones was a financial wizard. With a borrowed stake in 1902,
he had started a lumber business and run it into a fortune in downtown
Houston real estate. Through a maze of interlocking companies, he controlled the National Bank of Commerce, office buildings and hotels, insurance firms, investment houses, and a newspaper, the Houston
Chronicle. He seldom appeared as an officer or director in these companies. In fact, often he was only a name to the people who ran them
for him.

Somehow, during the thirteen years that Jesse Jones was in Washington, industries which could add stature to Houston just naturally

An oil barge in the Houston Ship Channel

owe, Jr.

seemed to gravitate in that direction. It was estimated that the government invested $300,000,000 in Houston's mighty chemical complex, and almost as much more in sundry other enterprises. The Brown Brothers, George and Herman, built 357 ships in Houston during the war.

Everybody thought the bubble would burst when the war ended. But instead it grew larger and more iridescent than before. The chemical plants expanded, meeting the postwar demand for new materials and fabrics of all kinds. While the oil industry settled down, and began to look elsewhere for fresh reserves, another volatile product of the earth around Houston came along to take its place. That product was natural gas.

Back in wartime, when fuel was desperately needed to keep war plants running, the RFC financed a pair of pipe lines, Big Inch and Little Inch, to carry oil overland to the East. They were built by George and Herman Brown, the same brothers who had turned out so many ships. Right after the war, in 1946, the Brown brothers rustled up a group of financiers in Houston and raised enough money to buy Big and Little Inch from the government for $143,000,000. They converted the flow from oil to natural gas, and organized the Texas Eastern Transmission Company to operate the system. Soon gas from Texas began to fire furnaces in homes and factories as far away as New England.

Natural gas has several advantages over other kinds of fuel. For one, it needs no treatment—it is ready to burn as it comes from the ground. For another, it gives off no smoke and leaves no waste—it is a perfect material for combustion. And it is relatively cheap, once the costly pipe lines are built.

Houston is the headquarters for half a dozen or more pipe line systems, conveying natural gas over the country. Besides Texas Eastern, they include the Tennessee Gas Transmission Company (next to El Paso Natural Gas, the largest in the country), Transcontinental Gas Pipe Line, and several smaller ones. All these companies have kept right on growing, while the oil business has been fretting about overproduction.

Another advantage of gas—from Houston's point of view—is that these businesses belong to Houston. Although they are publicly owned as a matter of necessity, since the investment is so enormous, their management remains in Houston. This is more than simply a point of local pride. It means that Houston is the financial center of the natural gas industry. By contrast, all the great oil companies with one exception— Continental—are controlled from New York City.

Of the older firms headquartered in Houston, by far the most renowned is the cotton merchandising house of Anderson, Clayton & Com-

Buffalo Bayou extension in downtown Houston

pany. Anderson, Clayton buys, sells, stores, and ships more cotton than any other organization in the United States or abroad. Its turnover seldom amounts to less than half a billion dollars a year, and on occasion has run as high as a billion and a half dollars. Doing business wherever cotton is grown or used, Anderson, Clayton has made Houston the principal cotton market of the world.

The privately owned Hughes Tool Company, founded by the father of its absentee proprietor, Howard Hughes, produces something like 80 per cent of all the drill bits used in oil exploration. More than half the rest are made by the publicly-owned Reed Roller Bit Company of Houston. Schlumberger, Limited, founded by a French physicist of Germanic stock, dominates the business of making geophysical surveys in oil formations. Wherever wells are drilled, "slumberjay" is a colloquial term. Pan American Sulphur, with mines in Mexico, and Duval Sulphur & Potash

Freighter loading at a dock on the Ship Channel

are growing competitors of the great Texas Gulf Sulphur Company, which has offices in both New York and Houston. Humble Oil & Refining, the operating affiliate of Standard Oil (New Jersey), is headquartered in Houston.

With a few notable exceptions—the most notable one being Jesse Jones—the men who made Houston what it is today were the kind who build or buy or discover material things, not those who merely handle money and investments. Take, for instance, Herman and George Brown.

They were sons of a storekeeper in Belton, up above Austin. Herman, the oldest, went to the University of Texas for a few months, gave it up, and got a job with a contractor in Temple, near his home. When the contractor went broke, owing Herman several months' pay, he took some building equipment instead of cash, and thus found himself at twenty-two in the construction business.

Meanwhile, George learned engineering at Rice Institute in Houston, went on to the Colorado School of Mines, and worked for a while for the Anaconda Copper Mining Company. Then he joined his brother. Herman had moved over to Houston shortly after the Ship Channel was opened, because that's where the most building projects were to be found. They organized the firm of Brown & Root, and developed it into one of the largest construction companies on the globe.

One reason the Browns have been so enormously successful is that they can and will build anything, anywhere. Ships and pipe lines during the war were only two inconspicuous items among their activities. They were prime contractors for American bases in Alaska, on the island of Guam, and in North Africa. They worked on the atomic-energy facilities at Los Alamos and around Santa Fe, New Mexico.

They have built offshore drilling platforms, dams, bridges, docks, highways, skyscrapers, and industrial plants. They own the Texas Railway Equipment Company, which carries on the world's largest salvage operation, not to speak of oil wells, an investment business, a dude ranch, and various other miscellaneous enterprises.

Much of downtown Houston is a monument to the creative energy of George and Herman Brown. Without them the city would most certainly have managed to get itself built, but just as certainly it wouldn't have borne the peculiar marks of bigness and enthusiasm which they have imprinted on it.

You might expect that a harbor as convenient as Houston's would be a fairly busy port of embarkation for Texas passengers traveling abroad, especially to the Mediterranean. By sailing from Houston, they

256 could save a long and tiresome trip to New York City, and at the same time add several pleasant days to the sea voyage. Besides, it would be in character for Texans to demand passenger service from their own ports.

A few years ago, the French Line had the same idea. With considerable fanfare, the new 20,000-ton liner *Antilles* arrived in Houston, took aboard a gay crowd of Texans bound for Europe, and sailed down the Ship Channel on her maiden voyage. The experiment was soon abandoned, just as the run from New Orleans to Le Havre in the *Flandre* had been dropped a year or two earlier, for lack of patrons.

For a time, the Italian liner *Francesco Morosini,* of 16,000 tons, touched more or less regularly at Houston on a rambling cruise that

S. S. "Antilles" sails from Houston on her maiden voyage

Mauric

started from Genoa and included stops at Barcelona, Lisbon, Tenerife, La Guayra (the port for Caracas), Curaçao, Habana, Veracruz, Tampico, and sometimes Brownsville. Ernest Hemingway once made an epic trip home from Africa in the *Francesco Morosini*. But that service has been cut off from Houston too.

The fact seems to be that most Texans on a holiday jaunt overseas prefer the superluxury of ships like the *Queen Elizabeth*, the *United States*, or the *Liberté*, that sail from New York. The only passenger traffic out of Houston at present is in freighters of the Lykes Line—the largest merchant fleet under the American flag—and various foreign carriers that put in occasionally for cargo. The accommodations aboard freighters are comfortable, informal, and easy on the pocketbook. They are popular with students and young married couples.

Maybe if the Brown Brothers built a superliner bigger than the *Queen Elizabeth,* and organized a company to operate it under the Lone Star flag, Texans would use it to go abroad. Meanwhile, they ignore the opportunity to book passage from Texas, and head east when they feel like an ocean voyage.

Though it lacks first-class facilities for sea travel, Houston does have its own transatlantic air service. KLM Royal Dutch airliners take off every day for Europe from the International Airport. Pan American provides flights to Latin America.

Of the little group of doges that included Jesse Jones, Will Clayton, and the Brown Brothers, few remain in Houston today. In most cases they have passed along the management of their interests to younger hands. But they have left no successors capable of inheriting their tremendous power.

For a while it looked as if Glenn McCarthy—widely heralded as "The King of the Wildcatters"—might be a figure worthy to succeed them. By coincidence, McCarthy was born the son of an oil-field worker at Spindletop, six years after the big blow-in. As a young man he was handsome in a rather menacing way. He married the daughter of a rich Houston oil man, and then proceeded—strictly on his own, and after the usual vicissitudes—to build an oil fortune eclipsing his father-in-law's.

At twenty-six, Glenn McCarthy was a millionaire. At forty he was being talked about around Houston as another Jesse Jones. He then owned—besides his own oil business—the Beaumont Natural Gas Company, a steel mill in Detroit, a chemical plant, a Houston skyscraper, an export-import business, a radio station, and a string of neighborhood newspapers which he was thinking about converting into another Houston daily. He lived in a splendid Colonial mansion that cost $700,000.

Refinery in Houston

Quincy

But there was a difference between McCarthy and such invisible titans as Jesse Jones or the Brown Brothers. He was given to spectacular gestures, and operated in the dazzling light of publicity. He flew around the country in a fleet of airplanes with a retinue of aides, patronized expensive night clubs in the company of a bodyguard, and vacationed in Mexico with Hollywood film stars.

The climax of McCarthy's career was the 1,100-room Shamrock Hotel, which he built on the edge of downtown Houston at a cost of $21,000,000. It was the finest resort ever seen in Texas, and one of the most magnificent anywhere. It had a swimming pool 165 feet long, fashionable shops and dining rooms, a medical clinic for ailing guests, and an enormous exhibition hall. Planeloads of celebrities and newsmen were flown in from Los Angeles, Chicago, and New York for the gala opening on St. Patrick's Day, 1949.

Within a year Glenn McCarthy's empire had begun to fall apart. Some of his properties were sold to satisfy creditors; some, like the Shamrock, were taken over by the insurance companies which had lent him money. The Shamrock now is operated by the Conrad Hilton chain. McCarthy went back to wildcatting in Venezuela and elsewhere. He has done well enough, but hasn't struck it rich again.

What did McCarthy in was not merely his flamboyance, or the fact that he confused the show of strength with its possession. Primarily, he failed because Houston has grown too vast—and has too much money invested in it—to be dominated by one man or coterie of men, no matter how grandiose their fortunes might be. Since World War II, Houston has entered a new financial incarnation. Today its outstanding figures are those who manage the wealth—in properties, cash, and institutions—left to their expert care by yesterday's giants.

Just in case there should be a citizen, here and there, whose portion of the bounty that is Texas isn't large enough to keep an investment counselor busy, Houston provides a home-grown mutual fund. Organized in 1949, Texas Fund is an open-end investment trust, specializing in stocks of companies that do business in Texas and neighboring areas of the Southwest. As of March 1960, some 13,000 small investors were subscribers to the fund.

It gave them an interest—worth about $36,500,000 at that time—in shares of eighty-six companies with which the well-being of Texas is inextricably linked. Basically, they consist of firms like Gulf States Utilities, Lone Star Gas, the Texas National Bank of Houston, or Southwestern Life Insurance, which are managed in that part of the world. But also

260   there are a few national companies of great renown, like Alcoa, Dow Chemical, Du Pont, or Standard Oil.

The officers, directors, and advisers of Texas Fund read like excerpts from a list of second-generation Texas financiers. The president is Clive Runnels, Jr., of an old ranching family. Some of his associates are John M. Bennett, Jr., a San Antonio banker; Lloyd M. Bentsen, Jr. (insurance); John H. Blaffer, whose folks were among the founders of the Humble Oil & Refining Company; William T. Carter, III, grandson of a Houston lumberman and banker; John T. Jones, Jr., president of Jesse Jones's Houston *Chronicle;* and former Governor Allen Shivers, now a director of quite a few Texas corporations, including Western Pipe Line (of which he is chairman of the board), Braniff Airways, and Texas Gulf Sulphur.

Almost all of Houston's outstanding institutions are legacies of men who made theirs, and then left it for the improvement of their city. The pattern was formed in the last century by William Marsh Rice, a merchant who hailed from Massachusetts.

Rice arrived in Houston in 1837, when it was less than a year old, as a young man without a dime in his pocket. Over the next half-century he managed to store up what was considered at the time an immense fortune in wholesale groceries and an export-import business.

In 1891, when he was seventy-five years old, Rice started an endowment fund for a college to be known as Rice Institute—because, he said, "Texas received me when I was penniless . . . and now . . . I recognize my obligation to her and to her children." When Rice was murdered in New York City nine years later, the endowment came to $5,000,000. It has grown since to more than $62,500,000.

Rice (now University) is one of the top scientific-engineering schools of the nation. Its enrollment is limited to not more than 2,000 of the most promising students in Texas. Its beautifully landscaped campus— often mistaken for the estate of some enormously rich oil man—is a Houston showplace, along with the handsome city park bequeathed by George Hermann, another early philanthropist. They border the main boulevard of Houston, between the business district and the Shamrock Hotel.

Equally impressive, in a different way, is the municipal University of Houston, on the other side of the city. It started as a junior college back in 1927, holding classes at night in a high school. By 1934 it had become a struggling senior college. Then it was taken up by the late Hugh Roy Cullen, an independent oil operator—originally from San Antonio—with the same feeling about Houston that had moved William Rice, and something like thirty times as much money.

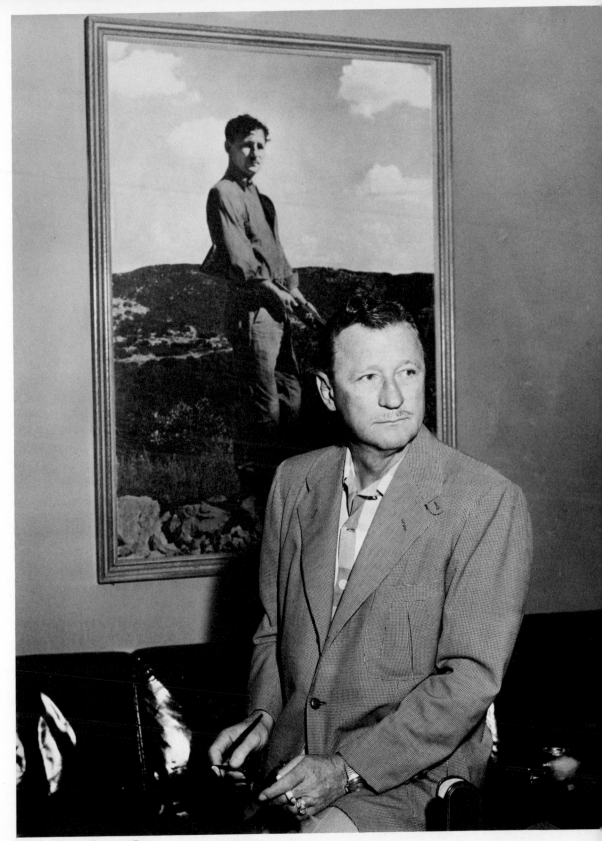

Glenn McCarthy, "King of the Wildcatters," in middle age

Statue of the founder on Rice University campus

Busy students throng the University of Houston

Cullen gave at least $20,000,000 to the University of Houston. In fact, he continues to support it, through the Cullen Foundation, which he set up ten years before his death to dispose of the proceeds from oil reserves valued as high as $160,000,000. The university now occupies a spacious group of modern buildings that provide lecture rooms, workshops, and recreation halls for almost 12,000 students. In Texas, only the university at Austin is larger.

Another imposing object of Hugh Roy Cullen's generosity is the Texas Medical Center, a collection of hospitals, medical schools, and

Cooksey—Houston Press

Part of Houston's vast Texas Medical Center

research laboratories spreading over 128 acres in midtown Houston. The center started off in 1946 with the Baylor University College of Medicine and three advanced medical units of the University of Texas: the Dental Branch, the Postgraduate School of Medicine, and the M. D. Anderson Hospital and Tumor Institute.

The M. D. Anderson Hospital—specializing in the study and treatment of cancer—was named for the late Monroe D. Anderson, one of the founding partners of Anderson, Clayton & Company. Through the M. D. Anderson Foundation which he left behind him, Anderson also has been a large contributor both to the Medical Center and to the University of Houston.

In the past fifteen years, the center has grown to include, besides the facilities with which it started, the Arabia Temple Crippled Children's Hospital and Clinic, the City-County General Hospital, the Houston Speech and Hearing Center, the Houston State Psychiatric Institute, the Methodist Hospital, the Texas Institute for Rehabilitation and Research, and the Texas Woman's University College of Nursing.

The older Hermann Hospital, next door to the center, has been enlarged and merged into it. Now in the blueprint stage are a Basic Research Building, a Clinical Research Building, a Jewish Medical Research Institute, a Lutheran Hospital, and a huge Good Samaritan Building to house staff and faculty members, students, and visitors.

Taken all together, the physical facilities will be worth close to $100,000,000. Even now, before the entire complex is quite completed, it has made Houston one of the world's major therapeutic centers.

No record of the families which have added luster to Houston can omit the Hobbys. Their case is all the more remarkable, because they have done it not by spending or giving away money, but simply by exercising personality and brains.

William P. Hobby was a newspaper reporter on the old Houston *Post* around the time of Spindletop. He worked his way up to managing editor, moved to Beaumont as publisher of a couple of papers there, got into politics, and served two terms as Governor of Texas during World War I. Afterwards, he went back to Houston as president of the *Post.*

In 1931, when he was fifty-four, Hobby married a young woman he had met in Austin, Oveta Culp. She was then a little less than half his age. Both handsome and smart, Oveta had been working for the Texas Legislature as an expert on parliamentary procedure. She joined her husband on the *Post,* and made herself so useful that by 1939 the Hobbys were able to buy a controlling interest in the paper.

**Golfers Jackie Burke, Jimmy Demaret, and Bing Crosby at
The Champions**

Quincy

Cattle on a bayou outside of Houston

Houston, the Metropolis

During World War II, Oveta Culp Hobby was on military leave in Washington as commander of the Women's Army Corps, with the rank of Colonel. She returned as co-publisher of the *Post*. In 1955, after another term in Washington as the first Secretary of Health, Education, and Welfare, she became the *Post*'s President and Editor.

From a rather sickly state when Governor Hobby first took charge of it, the *Post* has revived until it leads both the placid *Chronicle* and the *Press* in sales, and has the largest Sunday circulation in Texas. Oveta Culp Hobby is largely responsible. She has made it a policy to hire the best editors and writers she can find, and gives them a reasonably free hand. The result is that the *Post* not only tells the news, but tells it in a sprightly way.

The last time Mrs. Hobby needed a managing editor—in May 1960 —she didn't have to look far. In the city room she found her twenty-eight-year-old son, William P. Hobby, Jr., and gave him the job his father had held half a century earlier. Still another Hobby—Bill's wife Diana— runs the book section of the *Post*.

Houston, like the rest of Texas, is attracted by people with colorful or engaging personalities—provided they also know their business. When Dr. Efrem Kurtz in 1955 gave up his $30,000-a-year post as conductor of the Houston Symphony and went to Liverpool, England, the orchestra considered applications from a number of musical directors of great distinction, and turned them all down. Instead, it invited Leopold Stokowski —then in his early sixties, but a figure of tremendous verve and popular renown—to take the baton.

Stokowski accepted. His salary was said to be $50,000 for a season of eight weeks, conducting sixteen concerts. In addition he was entertained lavishly at the Petroleum Club, on top of the Rice Hotel, and in costly River Oaks mansions. But he gave the Houston Symphony the national attention it wanted.

In the spring of 1960 Stokowski announced that he would be retiring after one more season. The sponsors of the orchestra then faced a Texas-size, challenge—to replace him with a musician of equal glamour. They met it by cabling Sir John Barbirolli in Manchester, England. Sir John agreed to take over the Houston Symphony in the fall of 1961.

Houston is a city that provides more diversion for its own citizens than for visitors. It is a city of golf clubs—like The Champions, owned and operated by Jackie Burke and Jimmy Demaret—rather than the rodeos and stock shows that draw the country in to other Texas towns, though it has them too. It is a city where smart businesswomen meet in

268 private lounges for lunch, rather than one in which festive gatherings load their plates with tacos.

Its only tourist attraction of any note is in San Jacinto State Park— near the huge industrial suburb of Pasadena—on the battleground where Sam Houston and his homespun army won independence for Texas. There, in the base of a limestone shaft rising 570 feet above the prairie, is a museum housing relics of colonial and pioneer days.

There too, in a basin specially dredged for it, opening off Buffalo Bayou, is the battleship *Texas,* retired to its last mooring after valiant service in World War II.

Like most of the world's large cities, Houston is a rather impersonal place. Its mind is on the chemical plants along the Ship Channel—on the cotton market—on the ticker tapes in brokerage offices—rather than on making the casual visitor welcome. You go to Houston normally to transact business, not for relaxation. If pleasure is what you are after, you head for the coast, for the Hill Country, for the Big Bend, or the Valley.

It has been said that Houston has little in common with the rest of Texas. People who make this nostalgic observation may not have noticed that butadiene plants and skyscrapers are going up on the High Plains and along the Rio Grande, as well as in Houston.

The fact is that Texas has been passing almost imperceptibly into a new age of industrial development, leaving the legendary cattle era to the past. The plains are still there. But what we see in Houston is a profile of the face of Texas tomorrow.

For those of us who like Texas as it is, the new profile, lifting its towers against the all-enveloping sky, is at least as absorbing as the old one, with its look of timelessness and breadth. A land is to be used as well as admired. Factories are as much at home on the range as herds of Longhorns or buffalo, and a good deal more rewarding in the currency of the realm.

But there is room for both. Texas is nothing if not spacious. Its area is wide enough to encompass yesterday, today, and tomorrow, in one infinite expanse of time. And so it does, and so it will, for as long and as far as a living eye can reach.

INDEX

Index